D0119068

Reflections on Life

Reflections on Life

Science · Religion · Truth · Ethics · Success · Society

Walter Kistler

with Frank Miele

§ FOUNDATION FOR THE FUTURE, *Publisher*

© 2003 Foundation For the Future

Any portion of this book may be reproduced, by any process or technique, without written consent of the publisher.

FOUNDATION FOR THE FUTURE, PUBLISHER
123 105th Avenue SE
Bellevue, WA 98004
USA
www.futurefoundation.org

Library of Congress Control Number: 2003107332

Kistler, Walter P.   1918–

Reflections on life: science, religion, truth, ethics, success, society / Walter P. Kistler with Frank Miele.

Includes index.

ISBN 0-9677252-8-3 (casebound)

ISBN 0-9677252-9-1 (paperback)

1. Future – Humanity.
2. Science – Social Aspects.
3. Science – Philosophy.
I. Title.

First published in July 2003

Printed in the United States of America

To my wife, Olga,

for a lifetime of love, advice,

and counsel

Reflections on Life

Quotes from Walter Kistler

... there are laws beyond the realm of physics that control the matters of the mind ... they are just as implacable as the natural laws of physics or the logical laws of mathematics. PAGE 24

A problem arises whenever we insist that for a statement to be scientifically true, it must first agree with our opinion of what is ethically good. PAGE 47

Suppression of the truth will never last, regardless of any supposedly good purpose for which it is practiced. PAGE 51

We do not need the deceitful protection of the lie or someone to manage the truth for us. PAGE 52

We now have the ability and the responsibility to determine the trajectory along which our species travels through the third millennium. It is time we accept our responsibility to future generations and to the planet on which we evolved. PAGE 61

The concept of purpose does not exist in nature; it is entirely created by the human mind. PAGE 65

Quotes from Walter Kistler

Darwin's theory is not so much one of survival of the fittest, but of survival of the survivable. Over time, systems without internal discrepancies survive, while others that are in conflict with the demands of their environment disappear. PAGE 66

If anything becomes more and more evident for any thinking observer of nature ... it is that nature does not work on the concept of purpose. PAGE 69

[Heisenberg's] uncertainty principle freed our minds from the stranglehold of strict causality. The implications of this dethroning of causality ... are enormous. PAGE 69

Some of our best minds have given up and simply abandoned religion altogether. That's all right for them perhaps, but it exposes society as a whole to the poison of moral relativism. PAGE 70

The quirks and arbitrariness we observe force us to the conclusion that ours is not the only universe. PAGE 79

Most people, including many biologists, consider the creation of the first living cell to have been the critical, decisive step in the development of life on Earth. I disagree. I believe that this event was quite easy compared to the achievement of sexual reproduction. PAGE 87

A universe built by random forces out of chaos? Yes. PAGE 90

In a civilized society, children deserve the right to grow up in a stable, healthy family. PAGE 117

… changes in government, economic booms and busts, and military victories and defeats are only short-term ripples in the life of nations. The river runs much deeper. Nations reflect their people, rather than vice versa. PAGE 123

Acknowledgments

THESE REFLECTIONS on life would never have seen print if it weren't for the encouragement of my friends and colleagues, and the team that spent many months translating my Steno-script diaries into normal script. I owe a special thanks to Frank Miele, who took my translated reflections and put them into readable English. To all of you I am very grateful.

Contents

Preface

WALTER KISTLER

Scientist, Industrialist, Philanthropist

What we have to say is not adoration, not respect, not gratitude, though we have all those for him in great measure. It is simply to acknowledge that Walter Kistler represents the very best of humanity. The mind you are about to meet in reading these excerpts from his diaries is that of the most remarkable person either of us has had the good fortune to know.

— *Bob Citron and Sesh Velamoor*

BOB CITRON: When I first read part of Walter Kistler's diaries some years ago, I realized that they contained important comments on life and living that would be helpful to any thinking person who read them. Walter now has over 20 volumes of diaries that he has written during the past 60 years. Much of the content recounts his life experiences, but I think the most important parts of his diaries are his reflections on those experiences. This book is a distillation of some of Walter's best thoughts and ideas about the meanings he has found in his life.

Walter is a physicist and a chemist, and he has approached his life from a scientific perspective. While he has read widely about other approaches to reality, his life has been grounded in science, and his philosophy about humankind and the relationship between humanity and nature has always been science based.

Walter's comments reflect his beliefs of what it takes to live a productive life, a thoughtful life, a creative life, and a hopeful life. He has a lot to teach us. His words give us insight into the man and his thinking about the nature of the universe and our human place in it. His feelings about the human condition are the result of his life experiences as scientist, inventor, family man, businessman, and philanthropist. His words had the same kind of impact on me that Einstein's *Out of My Later Years*, Gandhi's *Autobiography: The Story of My Experiments with Truth*, and Bertrand Russell's *Essays* did in my younger years.

This book could have been entitled *Walter's Wisdom*, because the words are from a wise man whose daily thoughts and actions come from his rich experiences and his deliberations on the meanings of those experiences. Walter Kistler has had a profound impact on my own life and this book allows his views, his thoughts, and his ideas to be read by a broad audience. It will surely enrich the lives of those who read it for generations to come.

Bob Citron
Executive Director
Foundation For the Future
Bellevue, Washington
July 2003

SESH VELAMOOR: I have known Walter Kistler for 22 years. Together we have traveled extensively around the world, engaged in deep philosophical discussions, served on corporate boards, worked out in health clubs, and sat in living rooms and at dinner tables where we simply talked, one man to another.

An absolutely rare exception, Walter is the only person I know who has no vested interest other than in telling the truth and telling it like it is, and actually having a pretty good idea of *what* it is. His background is multidisciplinary; his interests are varied; and he brings a perspective that is not available to most people. His approach is a cold, rational, dispassionate perspective on the human condition that calls the lie, exposes the hypocrisy, describes the double standards, and is quite different from what you see from partisans who operate on a one-dimensional, narrow-minded basis.

Walter carries a lot of credibility because he not only "talks the talk, but walks the walk." He conducts his life totally and completely in accordance with who he is and what he believes. Walter Kistler is an exceptional and wonderful role model for anyone to understand and emulate.

Sesh Velamoor
Deputy Director
Foundation For the Future
Bellevue, Washington
July 2003

Introduction

Reflections from my diaries

THE MID-1930S was quite a time. Europe had recovered from World War I and was riding high. The horrors of Hitler and Stalin were only beginning to emerge, and few at that time discerned the abyss into which they would soon plunge not only Europe, but the whole world. Terrific scientific and technological advances concurrently occurred. As a result many of the best minds turned to philosophy, trying to explain the meaning of all this amazing new knowledge in physics, astronomy, and in technology. It was in those heady days that I developed an intense interest in science and technology, an interest and excitement that have stayed with me throughout my life.

I wanted to understand why things are the way they are, what makes the world tick. At the time I began my university studies, I started keeping diaries in which I recorded my thoughts and questions about every new subject I learned. This became a habit that stayed with me all through my life. This book is based on excerpts from those diaries, spanning a time of some 60 years.

To better explain what these diaries are all about, let me present some general facts here:

The amount of knowledge that science has since accumulated is incredible. And more and more is generated every year, every week, and every day. It is far more than any human brain can grasp. The first step on the road to understanding is to order and organize all this information, creating a system around which this enormous wealth of facts and figures can be arranged. That is what Linnaeus, the father of biological taxonomy, did by systematizing the inordinate number of plants and animals found on this planet. Only then could botany and zoology start on the road to becoming sciences. And only then could Charles Darwin develop a theory that could explain this organization in terms of science rather than theology.

There is a big difference between just knowing many facts and understanding the relationships between and among them. In the German language, *kennen* and *wissen* are two distinct verbs. *Kennen* means to know a person's name, or his address, or some other fact, while *wissen* means to know in the sense of understanding. The confusion between mere knowledge of facts and true understanding of the processes that explain them, however, goes much deeper than linguistics and is not limited to the English-speaking world. One of my goals in writing this book is to distinguish between *kennen* and *wissen*.

In many people's minds, knowledge is like a flat map. What is lacking is the third dimension, the *why* – the relationship a certain fact has to the world. The conventional two-dimensional map must be replaced by a relief of the countryside, one that shows not only distance, but the mountains and the valleys as well. Otherwise, as any hiker, or military planner, or surveyor knows, what seems like the obvious and easiest path may in fact be the path to failure or even disaster. Only when the relationships between facts are placed in the proper context can things be correctly deduced and understood for what they are.

The excerpts from my diaries are my attempt to draw such a three-dimensional map. I want to present the reader with a panorama of knowledge and ideas, and I will try to show some deeper relationships that, I feel, are not generally understood or accepted today. I also hope to shed some light on some important controversial questions concerning the world in general and human life in particular.

When I began keeping diaries I had no thought of ever publishing excerpts. It was simply my way of keeping a record of the thoughts and ideas that seemed important to me at that time. Only in the 1990s, over 50 years later, when I had them transcribed and shared them with some colleagues did their enthusiasm for what they read encourage me to do so. Given their response, I felt it would be worthwhile to have a lifetime of reflections recorded in a book.

For over 60 years now, from that day in 1939 when I started keeping my diary to the present, I have continued to read and think in the fields of physics, astronomy, chemistry, and biology in search of unadorned truth. I began keeping my diaries to record these efforts to obtain a better understanding of the world we live in, its workings, its ways and means, the *why* and the *how*. This book is a record of that lifelong endeavor, my intellectual odyssey from *kennen* to *wissen*, from knowing to understanding, which I now want to share with you.

Walter P. Kistler
Seattle, Washington
July 2003

1

The Laws of the Mind

PSYCHOLOGY TODAY is less like physics, even the early physics of Newton, and more like the medicine practiced during the Middle Ages. It is an important *art* that meets – or tries to meet – important human needs. It has accumulated a great deal of specific information and developed many therapeutic methods, most of them unsuccessful. Controversy remains, even (indeed especially) about the most basic questions. The main concepts are still largely based on wishful thinking, and what is taught by universities to their psychology students is based on outdated views.

When psychology has allied itself with established fields such as biology, genetics, and statistics, psychology has achieved scientific status. But these accomplishments are usually too limited and too abstract to address the everyday questions that people care about most. When it comes to giving our lives purpose, to making them more fulfilling and productive, psychology floats in thin air, devoid of any solid scientific basis or foundation.

This need not be. There must be basic laws, basic relationships governing matters of the mind just as there are basic laws governing the field of physics. The reason they have not been recognized is not for the lack of tools, the way a microscope was required to detect bacteria before we could discover the basis of infectious illnesses. Psychology needs few, if any, physical tools. It just needs to cease indulging itself – and its patients – in wishful thinking.

Psychology does not deal with neutral, inanimate matter, but with humans, with people who all have their prides and their sensibilities. In order not to offend them, certain things are not to be said, nor are certain areas to be investigated. The science of psychology is therefore surrounded by a minefield of taboos. Only a few courageous souls have dared to venture into this minefield, and they have had to pay dearly for their temerity. At least they were able to gather some very valuable facts and contribute to upgrading psychology from an art to a science. This is an encouraging start.

Based on experiences gathered over a long life, on my own feelings, and on the experiences of friends, as well as lots of reading and thinking, I have come to recognize some basic relationships in the realm of mental processes. It is my belief that there are laws beyond the realm of physics that control the matters of the mind, and that they are just as implacable as the natural laws of physics or the logical laws of mathematics. Failing to recognize or trying to transgress them can have serious consequences – just as serious as failing to balance your income and expenditures. It may take a while, but sooner or later, you will collide with reality.

The First Law of the Mind
The balance of pleasure and pain

I call the relationship of pleasure and pain the first law of the mind. What does it mean? It means that over the course of the life of any individual – and presumably any other animal as well – there is a net balance between pleasure and displeasure, between pain and joy, and over the lifetime of an individual this net balance is likely to be zero.

Just like those wishful thinkers who tried so hard to build perpetual-motion machines or the alchemists of the Middle Ages who tried so desperately to transmute base metals into gold, so millions of people today try just as desperately to create pleasure through chemical means such as drugs or alcohol.

Despite the short-term euphoria that can be induced by such quick fixes, in the long run those who repeatedly turn to them don't succeed and never will. Why? Because it takes pain to create pleasure and it takes hardship to achieve satisfaction. Life without hardship would not be utopia; it would be an eternal stupor. Hardship is required to keep the world going. There is no way to buy lasting happiness or comfort through money, but only through hard work.

The happiest people are those who aim toward a goal and, through hard work, have the satisfaction of making progress until they achieve it, overcoming the obstacles they know must arise along the way. The unhappiest are those who drift through life aimlessly, bereft of any design, plan, or objective. Over the course of their lives, both will experience about the same amounts of pain and joy, of pleasure and pain. When hard times come, as they inevitably will, the former group can reflect upon their achievements and draw inspiration from their past accomplishments as they can draw upon money saved in their bank accounts. The latter group can only look forward into emptiness – and they are the ones who are most likely to fall into depression or commit suicide.

The Second Law of the Mind
Conservation of motivation

The second law of the mind is the law of conservation of motivation. Though it is plainly visible, most psychologists, sociologists, and pedagogues either fail to see it or choose to deny it. This law simply states that, like energy and mass in physics, motivation cannot be created, nor can it be destroyed in an individual. You cannot create interest in learning, in sports, in people, in nature, or in the arts if the seed of that interest is not there to begin with. Why? Because, we now know, our drives, desires, and emotions do not reside in the cortex (the most evolutionarily recent and *highest* part of the brain that forms the surface area of the brain). They reside in the evolutionarily earlier, hardwired structures located deep inside the brain.

Education and upbringing have their effects on the cortex, which is like a computer and has memory. The inner brain, however, is relatively impervious to external influences. It is more like a controller, and one that is exceedingly difficult to program. That is the reason for the second law. Experience can direct the emotions to specific places, as research on identical twins has shown. But interest and intellectual drive have their origins in the fertilized egg; if they are missing, teaching will flow like water off a duck's back. Just as motivation cannot be induced where it is missing, it is also very resilient where it exists. Even a tough upbringing or a hard life will generally not destroy it.

THE THIRD LAW OF THE MIND
Nature × nurture, not nature + nurture

The third law of the mind concerns the famous and long-standing question about the roles of nature and nurture in the development of human abilities, personality, and interests. The law of nature × nurture simply states that the effects of nature and of nurture – that is, of inborn abilities and of upbringing – are not additive, but multiplicative. So, if either factor, nature or nurture, is missing, it cannot be made up by any amount of the other.

Like the first and second laws, the third law of the mind also runs contrary to the prevailing orthodoxy in social science and most of today's conventional wisdom. The third law is an especially bitter pill for the education establishment to swallow. What nature withholds from the genetic base of a newborn cannot be made up through any amount of education; likewise, without upbringing and education, even the genetically best-endowed person will be unable to live up to his or her potential. Neither Rudyard Kipling's Mowgli nor Edgar Rice Burroughs' Tarzan would be possible in real life, as convincing as they may appear to readers. *The Jungle Book* and *Tarzan of the Apes*, of course, were intended to be fiction. They were also written at a time when social taboos were not as strict, when a proud Englishman or Indian Brahmin could believe that the abilities of his race or caste would show up in his offspring under any circumstances.

A True Science of the Mind

I would hope that, taken together, what I have called the three laws of the mind – the balance of pleasure and pain, conservation of motivation, and nature × nurture – might provide a preliminary basis for a truly scientific psychology. They start with the premise that in the human (and the animal) mind, it is emotions – the feelings of pleasure and of displeasure, elation and depression, love and hate, kindness and anger, bravery and fear – rather than cold, calculating reason, that drive behavior. Without these emotions there is no human mind, no human intelligence, but only a computer.

While the laws of the mind provide answers to the real-life questions real people ask, they are incompatible with the dogma social science preaches, which most people today want to hear. As the second law makes clear, the task of parting with illusions and accepting reality in their place is not easy because it requires subordinating the drives, desires, and emotions that reside in the deeply hidden parts of our brain to our evolutionarily newer, computer-like cortex. And the third law tells us that this is inherently easier for some of us than for others, though a good upbringing in a society with solid ethical standards benefits all. But, as the next chapter will explain in detail, the first law of the mind is always there to remind us that, whether for individuals, families, groups, societies, or humanity in general, the momentary pleasure of illusions must always be paid back at some future time in equal amounts of displeasure, discontent, and pain.

2

The Balance of Pleasure and Pain

WHAT I HAVE presented as the three laws of the mind will require a lot more data, facts, and analyses so that they can be confirmed, modified, or rejected. This chapter will deal in more depth with what I like to call the first law of the mind because I consider it to be the most basic law. The second and third laws of the mind will not be described in any more detail. I am hopeful that these laws will stimulate further research in the future.

THE FIRST LAW OF THE MIND
The balance of pleasure and pain

To better understand how the first law operates, consider the well-known example of three bowls of water. The one on your left contains cold water; the one on your right, hot water; and the one in the center, lukewarm water. First, you place your left hand in the left bowl (cold water) and your right hand in the right bowl (hot water). After a few minutes you remove both hands and quickly place them in the center bowl (lukewarm water). To your left hand, the water in the center bowl feels hot, while to your right hand, it feels cold. While both hands are, of course, experiencing the identical physical temperature, the different perceptions are based upon the change from prior conditions.

A similar process holds true for our overall perceptions of pleasure and displeasure. After a while, the mind of the normal, healthy individual adapts to all but the most extreme conditions. That is why so many people who had lived a good life were able to survive the horrific experiences of concentration camps.

This law of the mind explains why, over the course of a lifetime, the level of happiness of someone living in wealth and comfort will not be much different from the level of happiness of a person living a simpler life. In either case, the mind adapts to the average level of pleasure and of pain, and only momentary changes are noticed. In other words, the experience of pleasure and pain is quantitatively the same for all humans. Only the range of circumstances that cause the pain and pleasure is different.

Returning to our analogy, the only way to maintain the perception of heat (or cold) is to place the right (or left) hand in increasingly hotter (or colder) bowls of water, until eventually we are placing them in scalding (or freezing) water. Likewise, the only way we can continuously experience happiness is by experiencing a series of ever increasingly good events in life, a very improbable and generally unhealthy state of affairs. So, over time, pleasure and displeasure tend to balance out.

Another example to explain the implications of the first law of the mind is the situation of a skier in the early days when ski lifts did not yet exist. In those days, anyone who wanted the thrill and enjoyment of skiing down a slope of, say, a hundred feet, had to first walk that same distance up the slope. Now imagine a skier with lots of money, more clever than wise, who offers his guide a large bonus to take him to a mountain site that possesses a very special topography that would enable him to leave the lodge in the morning, ski down the slopes and valleys all day, and then end up back at the lodge in the evening, without having to walk up even one step. Experience teaches us that such a *magic mountain* is the stuff dreams are made of, another perpetual-motion machine, a *something for nothing* scheme, that cannot exist in the real, physical world.

It is amazing that in spite of their lifelong experiences, so many people still haven't recognized the fact that there is no free happiness either. Just like the skier of old, before we can enjoy happiness we first have to earn it through effort and pain. The law of the balance of pleasure and pain is as implacable as the law of gravity that takes the skier downhill. Long recognized by the great minds in history as a fundamental fact of life, it was most poetically rendered in *Faust*, Goethe's tale of a man who so desperately desired one moment of total happiness that he sold his soul to the devil in order to obtain it. How many young people today who play with drugs and get hooked do exactly what Faust did? How hard it is for humanity to learn!

The Painful Truth about Pain

Over the course of time, the first law of the mind warns us, our feelings of pleasure and of displeasure must eventually balance out: experience a lot of one and we must later experience an equal amount of the other. Pursuing a state of perpetual happiness is therefore illusory and futile, because we will have to pay for every moment of happiness with an equal amount of discontent, displeasure, or pain. Rather than *pursuing happiness*, as such, we should pursue some goal and derive our happiness along the way from our accomplishments. Yes, there will be failures as well. There are always rocks on the road. But in overcoming those failures as best we can, we hone our skills and abilities, including the very important ability to tolerate frustration and learn from our failures, as well as personal skills in dealing with family, friends, and business when we are under pressure.

A major part of what is wrong with the developed countries today (definitely the United States and Europe, maybe not Japan, at least not yet) has its origin in this hedonistic philosophy that tries to violate the first law of the mind. The goal of trying to maximize pleasure and avoid pain is quite different from the attitude of past generations that made Europe and the United States great. In the long or even medium run, this self-indulgent philosophy can no more produce lasting pleasure and banish pain than can illicit drugs or overeating.

A great deal of the corruption we see in the Western world today also derives from this wanton search for instant gratification, for pleasure. In the olden days, the siren song of the pleasure principle was neatly balanced by the stern sermons of religion. Today, religion has lost its power to keep our lives on course. In its place, the gospel of self-gratification preached by many psychologists and sociologists, let alone the entertainment industry and its media pitchmen, tells us to "just go for it!" and "if it feels good, do it!"

The demands placed upon us by work have also lessened greatly. Enterprising businessmen, conscientious employees, and traditional families are still committed to hard work. And their reward is not only material, but the mental satisfaction that comes from a job well done or a love well earned. Sadly, however, far too many of our young people, students, children, and those who have been seduced into welfare dependency have acquired little or no sense of duty or responsibility. Rather, they feel free to indulge in alcohol, drugs, massive amounts of junk food, and sex without care or commitment, then wallow in idleness, and resent any attempt to chasten or chastise them.

At first glance, such a life might appear to be paradise on Earth – the socialist ideal achieved. But this is in no way paradise, because the first law of the mind forbids any lasting imbalance of pleasure and pain. Eventually the bill must be paid, the account settled, as equal amounts of displeasure, discontent, and pain are entered on the other side of the ledger in the form of lives ruined by drug addiction, failed marriages, broken homes, spoiled children, derailed vocations, mental breakdowns, and depression.

CLINICAL DEPRESSION OR SIMPLE SADNESS?

No amount of sex, no mind-altering drug, nor any amount of food, nor credit-card shopping sprees can ever free us from the first law of the mind. All those attempts to which some desperately turn in a vain attempt to *borrow* pleasure will eventually bring them only despair and then ruin. The happiest people are not the wealthiest, the ones judged most beautiful or handsome. They are those who, whatever their station in life, set a goal, and then have the satisfaction of making progress through hard work until they achieve it. The unhappiest are those who drift aimlessly with no goal in sight or mind, with no duty or purpose.

Depression is much more common today than it used to be, and suicide brought on by depression is a major cause of death. In my opinion, however, our society should be less reliant on antidepressants and other pills. Yes, there are mental disorders caused by genetic imbalances in brain chemistry that are best treated by a comprehensive program of therapy that includes prescription drugs. But if you compare the number of individuals in the United States being prescribed drugs and the number of new disorders and syndromes supposedly being diagnosed every day against the figures for other countries or our own recent past, something looks wrong. If we project those figures the same way we do budgets in economics or test results in engineering, America is headed toward a state where almost everyone will be diagnosed with at least one disorder or syndrome for which one or more drugs will be prescribed.

I suspect that there are many people who are not clinically depressed, but simply feel despondent, glum, or melancholy (as we used to say). From time to time, we all do. Here I can recommend a couple of very effective, very inexpensive, and very accessible remedies: fasting and physical activity. Try fasting for three or four days, eating nothing and drinking nothing but plain water, and see how those feelings of sadness or melancholy vanish. You will feel most miserable the first and maybe the second day. You will feel somewhat better if you use the time you normally spend for eating to go for long walks. The third and fourth days you will feel quite strange with a new outlook on life. What was very important before seems less important now. You will feel much less uncomfortable and the desire for food will have mostly disappeared. When you start slowly eating some food (preferably fruit) on the following days, your gloom and depression will be gone completely.

The other technique is some form of regular exercise or increased physical activity. The simplest and least expensive is walking. Substitute a good walk or riding a bicycle for driving while running some errand and see how it elevates your mood.

It is true that fasting and regular exercise are not always pleasant. They require making tough decisions and sticking to them. But often that type of discipline is exactly what *snaps* us out of feeling *blue*. Even cleaning up our office or house can *recharge our batteries* and get us going on the important tasks we have been avoiding. The worst thing we can ever do is to wallow in self-pity. Even in cases of true clinical depression, today's biologically oriented therapists recognize the importance of a healthy lifestyle that cuts out junk food and overeating, and substitutes an appropriate level of exercise, in addition to prescription drugs. And when we are not depressed but just sad, my prescription is: "Walk, don't eat; don't eat, walk!" It's tough, but very effective.

The Futile Pursuit of Happiness

The pursuit of happiness is defined as the ultimate goal in today's morality. This quest for self-gratification is not only futile, but disastrous, far more corrosive and destructive than its benign appearance would ever lead you to suspect. It is another one of the ill-founded, misleading concepts that are so often dispensed by social philosophers and politicians. Older generations understood that happiness is an elusive thing: Seek it and you will never find it; give it no mind and it will come to you on its own.

In the old philosophy of duty, of religion, and of hard work, the purpose of life was not the pursuit of happiness. None of the great religions of the past was based on such a view. To the contrary, they demanded solemn vows of asceticism and self-discipline, and the renunciation of the base pleasures of this world.

Nor was the pursuit of happiness the credo of past civilizations when they were at their peak; rather its appearance announced their impending demise. The pursuit of happiness was not the watchword during those many days when Rome was built; only during those of decay did *bread and circuses* become the slogan. The great philosophers of ancient Greece devoted their lives to the search for wisdom; medieval monks committed theirs to acts of faith; the thinkers of the Enlightenment pursued reason; the scientists and industrialists who gave us the modern era dedicated themselves to progress in science and technology. None pursued happiness as an end in itself.

The pursuit of happiness is a philosophy of deceit because it seduces those who would follow it with false expectations that entice them deeper and deeper into the pit of Hell – not Hell after death, but Hell on Earth, in this life. This self-indulgent philosophy gives rise to the practice of permissiveness, which, in turn, is responsible for the epidemics of drug abuse, sexually transmitted diseases, broken homes, out-of-wedlock births, welfare dependency, suicide, and many other evils that plague today's society.

The balance of pleasure and pain is a basic truth that the ancient cultures and religions understood when they preached self-discipline and looked down with contempt on the many pleasures this world offers. We, children of the modern age, cannot live like the ancient ascetics. A life of asceticism and renunciation would be flat, sterile, and unproductive. We want to enjoy the richer, fuller life this world offers. Well-earned times of rest, celebration, and interesting vacations help make life worth living, for ourselves and for others. But we must always be aware that we must do so in a measured way, mindful that at some later date we will have to pay in displeasure, hardship, and pain for each and every moment of enjoyment we borrow. The demands we make on ourselves for performing hard work, accomplishing a demanding goal, and honoring our commitments, on the other hand, will be rewarded, as they are entered as credits on our pleasure-pain balance sheet.

PROGRESS AND THE DRUDGERY OF WORK

Progress, of itself, has not led to more – or less – happiness; it has only given us the opportunity to lead more sophisticated, fuller, more interesting, and more active lives. Today, when the only purpose of life is the immediate satisfaction of all our desires, all work is seen as drudgery to be avoided. So, as each new machine or gadget enters the marketplace, it is advertised as a brilliant new invention that will "unburden us from the drudgery of work." Food comes prepackaged and precooked, dishwashers do the dishes. In addition to automatic washers and dryers for the home, there are laundry services that pick up and deliver. And so it goes. Are we really happier? I don't know. If we use this time productively in hobbies, reading, walking, or just being with our families, probably so. But what about watching television for eight hours in a row or sitting idle? That is not only boring, but unhealthy.

One thing I know for sure is that in the olden days people did not talk about the drudgery of work; they talked not only of the necessity, but also of the beauty and satisfaction of work. In our English lessons in Swiss schools, we learned the verses: "Work, work, my boy; be not afraid; look labor boldly in the face," which I still remember to this day. I do not know whether this is taught today in American schools. There is no drudgery in honest, productive work, no matter how humble. Rather, there is a physically and mentally healthy reward: the enjoyment of a rest well deserved for a job well done.

THE POWER OF POSITIVE THINKING AND SELF-ESTEEM

Much has been made of the power of positive thinking, and there is certainly a lot to it. Yes, we should attack all tasks that are mentally, physically, and ethically wholesome with optimism and enthusiasm, not fear and loathing. A positive attitude makes work more pleasant and success more likely. Today, however, the use of positive thinking has been oversold, and, like any good thing, too much of it has proven harmful to our societal health. Even more destructive has been the related concept of self-esteem. A cadre of social psychologists has brainwashed many parents and teachers: "Make sure children get everything they desire; deny them nothing. Don't rank them in school. Always be positive! And above all, never, ever, do anything that could possibly damage their self-esteem!" The result of this nonsense has been a couple of generations of emotionally immature, selfish, and self-centered children. (Fortunately, many do find themselves later in life, especially when they leave the overly protected nest and enter the cold, cruel, real world.) In a family, a school, a business, or a society where nobody is supposed to experience any hardship, eventually everybody will suffer in one way or another. The laws of the mind tell us that, like happiness, self-esteem is neither the secret of success nor an end in itself; it is the by-product of a job well done, a day well spent, a commitment well honored.

IMPORTANCE OF SELF-DISCIPLINE

Life without hardship would not be utopia; it would be an eternal stupor. Hardship is required to keep life going. Not only is nature full of hardship, but cruel death as well. Today's social activists think they can abolish cruelty, hardship, and pain, and construct a world that's all sweet and neat, where there is no poverty and no disease. They are not yet sure if they can or want to eliminate death altogether, but this would be the logical conclusion. They must think they are smarter than nature.

For humanity to survive, we will have to learn to discipline ourselves, to accept the inevitability of pain, and to view work and hardship not as obstacles to our immediate gratification, but as opportunities for greater achievement. Why? Because, like the skier of old, we can no more escape the laws of the mind than we can escape the laws of physics.

3

The Meaning and Value of Truth

WHAT IS TRUTH?
Truth is the unbiased interpretation of facts.

In a court of law, there are normally two opposing parties, both of whom think (or at least pretend to think) that their position is the truth. How can you tell? Maybe both are right or maybe both are wrong. The decisive factors here are the facts and interpreting those facts: interpretation that is free of the interpreters' biases, prejudices, and ideologies. The truthful interpretation is the one that takes all facts into account and agrees with all of them without any internal discrepancies or contradictions. However, pertinent, decisive facts are not always easy to come by and this is where the problem lies. Often, only scientifically correct investigation can get the facts straight, and that is why the scientific method is so important and should be the deciding factor in gathering facts.

Just as the world is not all beauty and glory, neither is the truth, the plain straight truth, always pleasant and uplifting. Often it can be discouraging to hear and, at times, even harder to accept. This raises a dilemma: Should we always tell the truth, the whole truth, and only the truth, knowing that it may cause some people to lose hope? In a court of law, we are sworn to do so. But what about in everyday life?

I do not think that suppressing the truth is ever a good policy, no matter how well intentioned. Not so long ago, doctors felt that they should not tell terminally ill cancer patients the plain truth about their condition. This view was rejected when they realized that trying to fool their patients did more harm than good. The doctors learned a basic truth: No matter how great their technical expertise, they were not all-knowingly wise, nor were their patients fools.

Individuals or groups can derive power from making statements that they pretend to be the truth and that they expect others to accept without question as the truth. Groups who are in power very often remain there by demanding unquestioning adherence to some fundamental religious creed or political doctrine. This was the case in the past, and it is the case in certain areas today. The Church in the Middle Ages, the Absolute Monarchs, the Nazi and Fascist regimes, and, until recently, the Communists in Eastern Europe, each had its own version of *the Truth*, which no one could question. And they all had their taboos, of which no one dared speak. Doing so could mean ostracism, imprisonment, or even death.

The traumatic experience of two awful world wars has brought a certain philosophy of skepticism to the Western world. In the old days there were taboos about sex, lying, and stealing. After Marx and Freud, we don't have any more taboos about sex, and lying is considered an excusable means, justified if it serves a *good* cause. Today many young people have abandoned the old religious morality and adopted the view, which has taken on semi-official status at many universities, that there is no good or bad, no up or down; everything is relative and just a matter of how you look at it and who looks at it; even truth is relative. Criminals are criminals because conditions made them so, or because of society. Genes have nothing to do with our behavior. All individuals, groups, and peoples are born exactly the same.

The boundaries between politics, science, and religion have become somewhat blurred. This is a dangerous situation, just as dangerous as it would be if the strict separation of the executive, legislative, and judiciary powers in a democracy were abolished.

The *soft* sciences of anthropology and sociology seem to be confused about their purpose and duty. Is their mission to do science, or is it to do good? Is it to tell the truth, or is it to work for what they judge is a better world? The latter seems to have taken precedence over the former. Social concerns are clearly their overriding consideration. And this bias or spin permeates all of the so-called scientific work that they produce. It ranges from distorting the facts as observed to omitting facts that are inconvenient and don't fit the bias.

Slogans like "all men are created equal," "there are no human races," and "only the environment counts" form the backbone of their science. Truth may be relative, but the slogans are absolute. Nobody dares question them or even discuss them. Political correctness has been elevated to a religion. Like all religions, it is motivated by good intentions; its assumptions, however, are questionable.

It does not much depend on what you say but how you

say it. Truth, however, does not make any value judgments; it does not say, "This is good; that is bad," or "This person is better than that person." It simply tries to state facts and their relationships correctly. Knowing the truth is always preferable, even for the terminally ill patient.

There has never been a time when recognition and dissemination of the truth defined as facts and their unbiased interpretation have been more critical. The tremendous scientific and technological advances made in the past century have given humankind awesome powers, which we have recklessly used for short-term gain without regard for the long-term damage done to our environment. Similarly today, with the best intentions, we are using our newly acquired power and wealth blindly without any knowledge about how we may affect the long-range future of the human species on this planet. Without thorough research, without knowing and disseminating the truth about human behavior and its causes, we will never know how our actions today may affect the lives of our children and our children's children.

Scientific Truth

Scientific research is a constant battle between different theories and hypotheses, where the better ones are determined not by revelation or our desires, but by how well they conform to reality. Scientists test their theories by performing experiments that are capable of disproving them. A good scientific theory should reflect reality so well that it can predict the outcome of a new experiment. One of the best-known examples is Einstein's Special

Relativity Theory. No matter how much the idea that a ray of light would be bent by a gravitational field went against the then-established views in physics, the theory was accepted by the scientific community when experiments proved not only that the ray was bent, but that the amount of curvature was exactly as predicted.

A problem arises whenever we insist that for a statement to be scientifically true, it must first agree with our opinion of what is ethically good. Such reasoning reflects a total ignorance of what science is all about. It fails to distinguish between what is objective and what is relative. Scientific truth is, by definition, objective. It may change based on new discoveries or experiments or methods, but it does not depend on who performs the experiment, how we look at it, or how we would like it to come out. There is nothing relative about it.

Our value judgments, on the other hand, are relative. We should never make value judgments in science. That is what has hindered scientific progress in sociology and psychology. They are too much influenced by opinions and value judgments. While our value judgments are relative, their consequences are not.

RELIGIOUS TRUTH

The difference between science and religion is that religion builds on a foundation of certain fundamental *truths* to be taken at face value and never questioned: People are all creatures of God and therefore sacred, and all of them are equal. Science is based on the premise that everything must be questioned and its validity proven again and again.

Religion is not science; it is not information. It is a call to action, a set of rules that define what type of behavior is permissible and enhances the cohesion of society. While they weren't based on science, the old religious views did reinforce strict rules of conduct that clearly differentiated between what was considered good and what was considered bad behavior. It has proven very useful for a society to implant certain beliefs that, whether right or wrong, mold the individual in a given way and prevent him from doing things that would hurt others and would weaken the cohesiveness of the society or threaten its survival.

According to the old Christian beliefs, bad people went to Hell, while good people went to Heaven. Even two or three generations back, our grandparents lived by rather strict rules of conduct; there was a clear-cut difference between good and bad behavior.

In Pedis Veritas

I think a person has to be very mature, have lived long and fully, possessed influence, and experienced a lot to fully appreciate that ethical behavior is much more than something pretty, just a decoration. It forms the fiber in the fabric of society, the skeleton in the body. It is essential for the success and long-term survival of a family, a business, a society, and the future of our planet.

In terms of society's code of conduct, I propose that there are some simple, quite down-to-Earth ways to resolve the problem of what is true and dispel the nonsense of moral relativism. First, just ask those proponents of relativism how they would like to live back in the age of the cavemen and freeze in winter, eat raw meat, see many of their children die of disease and themselves likely to die miserably at the age of 20 or 30. I bet they would be in deep trouble just giving up their air-conditioning or television. At least they would have to admit that a difference exists between good and bad as regards the material things of life. And if *one is as good as the other*, would they go back to the other?

There is an old Latin proverb: *In vino veritas* ("in wine [inebriation] there is truth"). I would like to suggest another such proverb to elucidate questions of ethics, economic and political systems, and the differences between nations, peoples, and societies in general: *In pedis veritas* (loosely, "we tell the truth through our feet"). We may not always see the facts and what they mean correctly. If we do, we may be hesitant to utter them. But we certainly seem to display a knowledge of the truth, without it being distorted by slogans and politically correct thinking, when we decide to move, often over great distances and sometimes at great personal peril, between one economic and political system and another, between one nation and another, or even between one neighborhood and another.

There is one objective, clearly measurable fact that allows one to declare one nation to be more successful or a better place to live. Just as water unerringly indicates which of two places is lower by flowing toward the lower places, so people indicate which is a better place to live by drifting toward it. During the Cold War, people in Eastern Europe risked their lives to cross the Berlin Wall and get to the West. They knew very well where the better place to

live was. Today, coming to the United States is the dream
of many people all over the world. Yes, there is a better and
a worse code of behavior; there is a rank order of political
and economic systems, and of the nations of the world.

MANAGING THE TRUTH

The ultimate irony is that those who most preach the gospel of moral relativism are also the ones who act as the
strongest censors on behalf of their dogma of political-
correctness. In today's America, there are two institutions
that try to manage the interpretation of facts, calling it
truth, and thereby influence what we think, the actions of
our government, and the decisions of our courts. They are
academia and the media.

The schools, colleges, and universities mold the thinking and opinions of the future generation, especially the
intelligentsia. The media in the United States are supposed to present all sides and all points of view. And to an
extent they do. But by accentuating the bad side of certain
events, while ignoring their other aspects, the media can
raise strong emotions, which can totally distort our perception of the true situation.

Then there are the taboos. Certain obvious facts, certain important truths are suppressed. Increasing levels of
censorship are required to keep us from speaking, writing, or even thinking the truth.

The would-be managers of the truth have a deep-
seated fear that the very fabric of our society would dis-
integrate if the truth, the whole truth, and only the truth
were known. In other words, academia and the media do

not trust us. They believe we are so immature that certain truths must be kept from us.

Our democracy is based on having the citizens decide. To do so, we need to know all the facts and have all the information. But if government, or academia, or the media decide they have the wisdom and power to "manage" the truth because we won't be able to handle it, we have no democracy at all. That is not only an insult to our intelligence; it is also a reckless sham.

Suppression of the truth will never last, regardless of any supposedly good purpose for which it is practiced. Eventually, it is bound to lead us into deep trouble. It is not the knowledge of the truth, but false, emotionally tainted ideas that have led past generations down the road to violence, war, and environmental destruction. And this is exactly what will happen again if we continue to close our eyes to our many problems and pretend that everything is for the best in order to preserve the cherished illusion that this is the best of all possible worlds.

Sure, it would make life easier and simpler if the ostrich stuck its head in the sand and pretended that the lion could not see it and that it didn't see the lion approaching. But it wouldn't be simple for very long – which is why even ostriches don't really do that.

THE IMPERATIVE FOR TRUTH

This century's enormous advances in science, in technology, and in medicine have given us immense power over our environment and our destiny. Our understanding, however, of the consequences of our actions on the long-range future of the human race and on our destiny seems totally lacking. It is imperative that we understand the true effects of the power we now have. Willful ignorance can no longer be excused. I believe that even the most sensitive issues must be thoroughly studied, investigated, and openly debated. We do not need the deceitful protection of the lie or someone to *manage* the truth for us. Humanity must be enlightened enough to accept the facts of life and live with them, and civilized enough to behave like humans.

4

The Meaning of Success

WHAT DEFINES success? The first things that usually come to mind are wealth and free time to spend as we like. But wealth and leisure are the result of success, not the cause. In many cases, unearned wealth and leisure can undermine success.

There is a law in physics that says: Given an empty container, a gas will expand and take over any volume that is offered to it. There seems to be a similar law related to money and work in human affairs. An individual, a family, a company, a society, or a nation can readily absorb all the money it is offered, avoid all the work it can avoid, and still complain that it is not getting enough money and has too much work. Unless checked, we have the capacity to spend whatever free time and wealth technology brings us.

Today's Western world has it better than ever. Young people who have everything given to them are often unsuccessful. They often cause suffering not only to themselves, but for their parents and for children they thoughtlessly bring into the world.

The thought of a perfectly peaceful society where everyone is wealthy and has lots of leisure may seem attractive, but it would be boring and stagnant. Tension, pressure, and internal conflict are required for progress. But they must be reined in by a solid ethical system.

If wealth and leisure do not define success, what does? I remember asking several friends to name the most important considerations in selecting the region or country in which they would most like to live. Was it the geography, the climate, the average income? After discussion, they were surprised at their conclusion: It was none of those; it was the people. When I asked top executives to name the most important component of success, they answered "attracting and keeping talented people." Clearly, the quality of the people we live and work with is the active ingredient that generates success.

A successful family, business, or society cannot exist without honest, knowledgeable, and industrious people. The formula for a successful society is to provide its population with the right upbringing, a functioning infrastructure, and a solid ethical system.

THE INDIVIDUAL

A successful individual is one who is intelligent, interesting, ethical, concerned about others, and dedicated. He or she is someone who can be relied upon in difficult times – in short, a person of character and moral fiber. Self-control is just as important as intelligence in determining success. A person of character controls his emotions and desires. He puts duty before freedom. Only proper education can teach that.

How we make use of our leisure time also plays a part in determining our future life outcomes. Successful children develop hobbies. Some build model airplanes and rockets. Others learn how to repair cars. Still others learn rock climbing, go on nature trips, sail, read books, collect stamps, or care for younger children and pets. Those without hobbies end up directing their youthful energy into self-indulgence, or even worse, violence.

THE FAMILY

Successful children usually come from successful parents. This does not mean parents who are materially wealthy. When I look at the young generation, I see that young people overall have a life that is good; in a material way, maybe too good. As a young man, I lived in a small rented room, wore simple old clothes, ate low-priced meals, and could just barely afford an under-powered motorcycle. Many of today's young people, however, have all the clothes, food, cars, and electronic devices one can imagine.

Good parents are not those who give their children everything. They are those who exercise judgment and determination in supervising their children's education. They must be willing to devote lots of their time to them, rather than being mere passive observers. Parents should set aside time to read to their children when they are very young and then guide them in the books they select as they learn to read on their own. Parents should plan their weekend activities (like sports, biking, visits to museums) and vacations around being with their children, not getting away from them.

However, parents must also care enough about their children to be willing to correct them when that is needed.

Hardship and work develop character and make for a balanced, happy life. Discipline should be used only if it promotes a desire in the children to overcome obstacles and encourages them to strive, to fight, to work harder for what is better. Parents can do that only if they know each child's limits. We are not all identical. What tempers the character of one child can crush the spirit of another.

THE VALUE OF TRUST

Having enough people with high ethical standards is essential for the successful functioning of a society where life is satisfying and worth living. Therefore, supporting these families should be one of society's most important concerns.

A successful society is built by people who are honest and reliable, and who seek to do the right thing. They must be generous people, ready to help others truly in need. Criminal behavior does not even enter their minds. A society built on trust can function efficiently on just a promise and handshake. Where trust is absent, we have to rely on lengthy contracts, formal rules, bureaucracy, and litigation.

Many Third World countries have abundant natural resources and hard-working people, but they are not successful. Their enormous bureaucracies paralyze free enterprise. Doing business there means hours just filling out forms. The real killer of efficient business transactions, of incentive, and of dedication is corruption. Any business or country in which corruption prevails will never, ever achieve lasting success.

Our propensity for trust and voluntary association permitted the United States to emerge as the world's premier economic power. America as we know it would quickly stop functioning if it were not for the many highly motivated people who work hard for a cause, and generally for a good cause, irrespective of whether it brings them any immediate gratification. That is what has made America great and still keeps it functioning today. But the decline in trust that has taken place in recent decades now threatens our economic future.

For more than a millennium, our Western world was guided by the tenets of the Judeo-Christian religion. In particular, the Protestant work ethic emphasized responsibility, hard work, honesty and dedication. This is what has created our great nation. Today this work ethic has been undermined. Colleges emphasize the role of ethics less and instead teach the art of creative financing, leveraged buyouts, and hostile takeovers.

Since negotiating and wheeling and dealing are easier than creating and producing, many of our most capable young people decide to become lawyers, stockbrokers, or real estate dealers rather than engineers or production managers. Suing has become a national pastime. We waste vast amounts of money on frivolous or hateful lawsuits, precarious real estate deals, fraudulent insurance claims, and unnecessary medical expenses. The vices of greed and self-interest are displacing the virtues of decency and respect as the American creed.

In the long run, being considerate of other people makes a society more successful, both materially and ethically. Treating everyone with courtesy makes life better for all. Only when we behave at such a high level do we rise from being merely human to being truly humane.

MATURE LEADERSHIP

Even with the best people and abundant resources, the people at the top can also make a difference between a successful nation or company, and one that stagnates or fails. They cannot just sit in their offices and *plan*. They have to get out, see the people, understand what they are doing, and show appreciation for what they have done. In a word, leaders must lead.

For a person of intelligence and ability, the highest performance in a key executive position comes at a rather late age. The age of maximum physical stamina is about 20 (typical for swimmers). Maximum physical performance and capability are not reached until about 30 (e.g., climbers); maximum intellectual performance, about 40 (e.g., professionals, doctors, lawyers). For a position that requires the highest levels of responsibility and authority, where judgment, intuition, and experience are critical, peak performance comes much later. Some of the greatest leaders in human history were well into their 60s at the time of their highest achievement.

GENIUS AND CREATIVITY

In a successful society, each generation must produce its share of scientific, artistic, and humanitarian geniuses. What characterizes the genius, the great innovator? A person can be very intelligent, work hard, understand his field perfectly, and still not be a genius. What makes the difference? A genius must have the courage to discard the rules of the game, the authorities, and the assumptions accepted in that field. He must think outside the box that confines even the best minds of his generation. He must have the courage to make his own rules, build a new base, and discard the old one.

True genius also requires the ability for selection and judgment. The creative person must be able to choose the one good, stable, and survivable path from a large number of possibilities. Next, he must be able to march down that path with zeal and energy. Then, he must have the tenacity and fortitude to stick with it through hardship, reversals, and disappointments all the way to the finish line. But a true genius must also be able to abandon a path he has chosen if it does not work out. He needs the courage to accept criticism and learn from his mistakes.

DILIGENCE AND DETERMINATION

Great scientists, leaders, and thinkers are critical to the success of a business or society. When things are going well, the president of the country and the congress, or the parliament, receive the praise. But neither the president nor the legislature can do much alone. What counts most are the people. Generally a government reflects the people. A corrupt government is more often the result, rather than the cause, of a lazy, careless, and corrupt population.

The same principles hold true in science and industry. A few great men get the fame and the credit. However splendid, their achievements would not be possible without support from many people and many institutions. It takes thousands of people getting up everyday, working hard, and doing their tasks with quiet dedication. A great scientist or great inventor cannot work from inspiration alone. He relies on a well-fitted laboratory, dependable communications, and a reliable transportation system.

All these things are possible only if there are machinists, service providers, and employees who are hard working and perform their duties reliably. Just as important are the dedicated, technically capable technicians and mechanics who repair our home appliances and keep our airplanes flying and our complicated production machines operating.

A well-functioning infrastructure and a dedicated work force do not only make our lives pleasant, they allow us to achieve more because we are free to concentrate on our jobs without having to worry that our cars may stall out on the way to work or that our flights to important meetings may be needlessly cancelled. America's human and technological infrastructure has given our farmers the technology to feed most of the world.

Ensuring a Successful Future

What do we want? Do we want the society of the future to be violent and aggressive, or harmonious and peaceful? Do we want future generations to be intelligent, hard-working, reliable, friendly, respectful, and caring, or ignorant, hostile, indolent, and resentful? Do we want them to live in a healthy environment with clean streets and neat homes, or in the midst of decadence, squalor, and decay? Do we want the society of the future to be one composed of competent service providers, incorruptible civil servants, and dedicated businessmen, or one riddled with avarice, corruption, and venality?

We have the choice and we must make up our minds. We now have the ability and the responsibility to determine the trajectory along which our species travels through the third millennium. It is time we accept our responsibility to future generations and to the planet on which we evolved.

5

Three Worldviews

Jesus, Darwin, and Heisenberg

You MAY wonder how I can, in one breath, mention three great men whose teachings seem totally unrelated, in some ways even contradictory. It is not because I am trying to repair the irreparable cleft between science and religion. The reason, rather, is that the teachings of the Christian religion, the theory of evolution, and the revelation of the uncertainty principle have influenced my thinking and understanding of the world more than any other knowledge I learned in my life.

There is great doubt that the gap between science and religion will ever be bridged, because the two reside in two different levels of reality that do not interact. Science addresses the questions of *what is* and *why it is*, while religions tell people how to behave in order to create a stable and, in their view, good society. The Christian religion especially asks that we love our neighbor, show compassion for the less fortunate members of our society, and help those in need. It also orders people not to lie, not to steal, and not to kill, and it has contributed a lot to help build better societies in which people help each other, trust each other, and work together more smoothly and efficiently. Religions also help people deal with their personal problems, giving them a goal to work for and hope for later reward for their efforts and good deeds.

However, the chivalrous view described above also contains the germ of self-destruction when it is gratuitously and unconditionally extended to those who cannot or will not live by it, or when it clashes with the cruel laws of nature. In the long run, nature will win; whether it is in our biology or in our cultures and civilizations, Darwin's iron law of survival still applies.

Furthermore, where religion has ventured into the realm of science, dealing with the material world and explaining what things are and why they are, it has run into deep trouble and has had to retreat every time.

The last 2,000 years of Western world history have seen repeated clashes between the Christian religion and our emerging knowledge of the physical world. As the laws governing the motion of the celestial bodies became understood, the ancient biblical views of, first, a flat Earth and, then, the Earth as the center of the universe had to give way to the astronomy of Copernicus and Newtonian physics. Then, as more and more of the biological past of our planet with its formations and fossils was discovered, the view of a seven-day creation also had to be discarded. The most crushing blow of all to our egos came from Darwin's theory of evolution, which shattered the myth of human uniqueness as a creature made in the image and likeness of God. Religion should not try to explain the world; it should limit its activities to telling people how to behave, giving guidance to those who need it, and giving sense to an otherwise empty life.

Religion is under strong attack today in our Western world, but it has been under attack for the last two hundred years since the French Revolution and since the Age of Enlightenment, and still it has survived. It appears today to be as strong as, or even stronger than, it was at the beginning of the last century. This certainly indicates that the human mind cries out for more than simple facts and science. The concept of purpose does not exist in nature; it is entirely created by the human mind. And the human mind needs a purpose for its actions. Humans are not computers and human thinking is far more than simple logic. Science can be exciting for some, but for most people, it appears cold and grey. It does not know any purpose and does not give any hope or meaning to human existence.

However, humans are motivated by emotions and drives, and hemmed in by worries, concerns, and fears. All these things don't exist in science outside the human mind. That is where the role of religion comes in: It gives life a purpose and hope. The Christian religion gives marriage a solid base and gives solace to the dying. Tougher minds with courage and strength may get along without religion, but the average person of today with sensitivity and strong emotions needs something more than science and will need it, in all likelihood, in the coming centuries. However, religion will have to retrench into its own realm, stop attempting to fight evolution with creationism, accept science as the realm of knowledge, and limit its concerns to matters of the human soul.

Most Eastern religions are much less specific in their descriptions of the world, less given to taking old legends literally, and are therefore better able to accept modern science. The Christian religion still has a long way to go to drop its claims to scientific truth and to stop interfering in the domain of science where it can never hope to prevail. The head of the Catholic Church made a decisive step in this direction by officially accepting the concept of evolution. Other Christian doctrines would do well to follow this example. This would make religion more acceptable to inquisitive minds. It is interesting to note that even great scientists like Newton, Pasteur, and Einstein relied on religion to give their lives more meaning, even as they helped to dismantle its most fundamental beliefs.

DARWIN
Survival of the survivable

Religious people often ask: "How could the world around us be so beautiful, so balanced, and so well organized without a Creator God?" My answer is one word: Darwin! I don't mean that Charles Darwin created it, but that his theory of evolution by natural selection explains how life developed. It even explains how the cosmos developed. Darwinism explains how and why systems become organized without the intervention of any supernatural organizer.

I first learned about Darwinian evolution from my older brother when I was eleven years old and quite religious. It made sense to me immediately and did not clash at all with what were then my religious views and what are still my ethical values.

Darwin's theory is not so much one of survival of the fittest, but of survival of the survivable. Over time, systems without internal discrepancies survive, while others that are in conflict with the demands of their environment disappear. That process, not some Creator God, is the reason that everything around us, from a little flower to a vast galaxy, is so orderly and breathtaking.

HEISENBERG
The cosmos does play dice

Darwinism can explain how the cosmos, life, and even the human mind changed and developed without the guiding hand of the Almighty. But it cannot answer the age-old question of where it all came from in the first place. The principles of classical physics such as conservation of energy and conservation of mass, or the principle of conservation of mass-energy in Einstein's relativistic physics, prohibit something coming out of nothing. Religious thinkers may accept some form of evolution, but they have one strong argument to support their beliefs. Since our universe does exist, they say it must have been created at some point. The Big Bang theory indicates that such a point does exist at a well-defined time in the history of the cosmos. How then can we explain the Big Bang itself without some Unmoved Mover to first set the whole process in motion?

This religious retort has one big flaw: It instantly raises the question, "Who created God?" It reminds one unpleasantly of the antinomy of the ancient Greeks:

— What supports the Earth in space and prevents it from falling down?

— Well, it rests on the shoulders of the giant, Atlas.

— But on what is Atlas standing?

— On a great turtle.

— But where is the great turtle resting?

— It's swimming on a great, wide ocean.

And so you can go on forever. The problem with the concept of creation arises from the quite natural assumption – or rather feeling – that the normal state of things is nothingness, an empty void, a clean, pure vacuum, in which God then created everything. It requires supernatural, superhuman intervention to create something from nothing.

It is here that Heisenberg made his decisive contribution: the principle of uncertainty.

Quantum theory's uncertainty principle tells us that a pure, clean vacuum cannot exist. What we would find instead is a state of chaos. Tensors of high energy may appear and disappear, sometimes interfering and creating strange things.

Another implication of Heisenberg's theory is the elimination of strict causality. This is a concept that runs completely against our feelings. Things, however, do happen without any cause, without a reason, just from simple probability. For instance, we know that electron-positron pairs appear and disappear "in empty space" all the time. Instead of the miraculous initial act of some Creator God, we see the repeated creation of mass and energy, randomly and without cause.

The same principle allows, indeed predicts, that larger things like universes would appear and then in most cases disappear instantly. Modern cosmology and astrophysics describe the creation of not *one* universe, but a seemingly infinite number of universes that appear and disappear like soap bubbles, of which only a very few survive.

The implications of Heisenberg's uncertainty principle for physics, philosophy, and our comprehension of reality exceed even those of Einstein's theories of special and general relativity. How deeply the concept of uncertainty offends the bias of our evolved minds is illustrated by Einstein's statement, "I shall never believe that God plays dice with the world." For all his genius, Einstein could never bring himself to accept quantum theory's uncertainty principle. It is somewhat surprising that such a great, iconoclastic mind was unwilling to accept another revolutionary worldview. Einstein simply could not accept the idea of randomness governing the universe. This may be due to his religious beliefs.

Randomness is the one thing the religious worldview cannot tolerate. If anything becomes more and more evident for any thinking observer of nature, however, it is that nature does not work on the concept of purpose. So, contradictions continue to arise whenever humanity tries to put purpose into a nature that does not know what purpose is. Human intelligence, not nature itself, created the concept of purpose.

The uncertainty principle freed our minds from the stranglehold of strict causality. The implications of this dethroning of causality from our mental pantheon are enormous. Things can happen without a cause. Laplace's demon, who, given the position and momentum of every atom in the universe, could then predict the future in every detail, has been exorcised.

Probability, not determinism, now governs the cosmos. And while the probability that a universe like ours could emerge from nothing is not very great, it is not zero either – and it has infinite time in which to happen.

JESUS
Teachings in ethics

It seems less and less believable that an omnipotent, benevolent God would have created our cruel, imperfect world. More and more clearly, modern science is revealing a world arisen from chaos through the driving force of randomness, guided only by Darwin's principle of survival of the fit and the nonsurvival of the unfit.

How, then, can we stay true to the ethical teachings of Jesus? Must we sacrifice all sense of the sacred on the altar of the scientifically verifiable? Some of our best minds have given up and simply abandoned religion altogether. That's all right for them perhaps, but it exposes society as a whole to the poison of moral relativism. Others have tried to cook up some ecumenical ragout, a moral mélange, incorporating what they believe are the best parts of every religion. But all religions are not the same. Many religions preach – and at one time or another, every religion has practiced – inhumane, destructive beliefs that are completely incompatible with the Sermon on the Mount. When Gandhi said he would gladly declare himself a Christian were it not for the examples he saw all around him, he was making a statement that can be applied to all religions.

Many, maybe most, Americans are so dedicated to preserving the Christian ethos that they are willing to warp science by making it conform to the old biblical worldview. They insist that life and the cosmos could not possibly be so beautiful, so balanced, and so well organized without a Creator God, an Unmoved Mover, or First Force. The problem here is that people like to see a simple world, a world located all on one plane where everything can be interrelated and everything can be understood by applying the same concepts, the same laws. Trying to mate science with religion or science with politics is like trying to mate different species of animals: It does not work. A true democracy keeps the three powers of government strictly separated. Once the lines of separation blur, a dictatorship or chaos is the result.

I believe that we can and must stay true to the two quests that have distinguished Western civilization from its inception: the search for truth and the pursuit of justice, ethics, and fairness. We must accept the duality of the teachings of Jesus and the theories of Darwin and Heisenberg without trying to reconcile them. We can then understand why the cosmos not only could, but indeed almost had to, arise out of nothing, and how survival of the survivable, not the guiding hand of an almighty God, directed the development of the universe, the solar system, planet Earth, life, and, finally, the human mind. At the same time we may accept religion as a creation of the human mind that addresses purely matters of the soul and not of the material world, giving people's lives a purpose and addressing their worries and concerns.

6

Cosmology

Before the Big Bang?

THE DISCOVERY in the 1920s that all the galaxies were speeding away from us led to the conclusion that the universe began at time-zero from the initial explosion of a single point of infinite density, infinite pressure, and infinite temperature: the Big Bang. Religious leaders liked the idea since it seemed to be compatible with a supernatural act of creation at a specific moment in time.

Some scientists were skeptical, however. For one thing, the best estimate then available of how fast the universe was expanding implied that the Big Bang occurred 1.8 billion years ago. This figure appeared highly problematic because radioactive dating techniques had shown that some geologic formations were much more than 1.8 billion years old. Who was right: the astronomers or the geologists? It turned out that the down-to-Earth geologists had the more accurate number. Did this mean that the Big Bang theory was wrong? No, because more accurate measurements of the rate of expansion set time-zero back to 10 to 15 billion years ago.

The theory still lacked any direct substantiating physical evidence, however. Physicists had computed that an important step would have occurred in the evolution of the cosmos when things cooled sufficiently that matter and radiation de-coupled. Up to that point, the cosmic temperature would have been so high that a continuous interchange between matter and energy (in the form of light) would have taken place and then suddenly stopped at this critical juncture. The radiation that filled the universe should still be there, but only in the diluted form of low energy photons (that is, longer electromagnetic wavelengths). The entire universe should still be bathed in microwave radiation.

Only in 1965, when Arno Penzias and Robert Wilson at Bell Labs confirmed the existence of this universal background radiation (for which they were later awarded the Nobel Prize in physics in 1978), did theoretical physicists feel sufficiently confident that they began developing detailed scenarios of the evolution of the universe, calculating its temperature, its density, and its composition way back in time to within seconds of its creation.

THE BIG PROBLEM WITH THE BIG BANG THEORY

There was still one big problem with the theory of the Big Bang: What happened before the Bang? Unless one invoked some Creator God to set it off, the Big Bang appeared to violate the most basic laws of physics, conservation of mass and conservation of energy. Einstein's equation of $E = mc^2$ had proven that matter and energy were really the same. (Destroy a minute amount of matter and you release a vast amount of energy.) So, there is really only one law, conservation of mass-energy, but the problem still remains.

The law of conservation of mass-energy is the most

basic, most absolute law in the whole universe. It never suffers any exceptions under any circumstances. Even a black hole that swallows anything it encounters, including a beam of light, does not make mass or energy disappear. The mass of the black hole simply increases by the amount of the mass (or energy) it swallowed.

How, then, could the laws of physics have allowed the creation of a whole universe with all its stars and galaxies? Can we imagine either nature or God starting the Big Bang, making something appear out of nothing, and then moments later instituting a universal, inexorable law, so absolute that nobody or nothing, not any exploding star nor black hole, could ever transgress it? That seems far too frivolous and arbitrary for either God or nature.

The resolution of this paradox grows out of Heisenberg's uncertainty principle. Quantum mechanics eliminates any need for metaphysics. The world of subatomic particles is not governed by cause and effect but by uncertainty. Here *empty space* is not a pure *vacuum* (that is, space totally devoid of any matter/energy), but a false vacuum, a chaos. *Emptiness* is just one of many possible states, and not even the most probable one. Rather than *the void* out of which God created it all, the uncertainty principle tells us that the pre-Bang chaos consisted of an indeterminate number of vacuum fluctuations that appeared and disappeared until one (or more) managed to survive.

Let's consider an analogy: We have a number of dice. Each one has six sides, with a different number engraved on each. But instead of the usual 1 through 6 found on gaming dice, ours are marked 0 through 5. We shake all the dice in a cup and toss them. Would we expect them all to come up 0? On every roll? Certainly not! Zero is just one possible outcome and since all the other values have an equal probability of 1 in 6 (i.e., .167), some nonzero result is five times more probable (i.e., 5 in 6, or about .83) for each die. If we roll two dice, the odds of getting a zero on both are $\frac{1}{6} \times \frac{1}{6} = \frac{1}{36}$, or about .03. If we roll the two dice three times the probability of getting only zeroes is $\frac{1}{36} \times \frac{1}{36} \times \frac{1}{36} = 1$ in 46,656, or about .00002.

In the case of the pre-Bang dice game, we don't know how many alternatives there were or how many dice. What we do know is that infinite cosmological time allows an unlimited number of tosses. With those parameters, a nonzero result (the creation of something, anything) becomes a virtual certainty.

THE NEXT STEP
Cosmic inflation

The principle of uncertainty makes it probable that *something* could appear out of *nothing*, but is it reasonable to think that all that we see around us could then develop from that little thing? Here, I believe, Alan Guth at MIT and Andrei Linde of Stanford University have given us the next piece in the puzzle: cosmic inflation.

While the theory is physical, not fiscal, the best way to get some understanding of the theory may be to look first at the workings of our capitalistic economy. Money is an absolute, a thing you cannot create out of nothing, at least not legally. Suppose a smart young engineer or scientist has a bright idea for a potentially profitable product, but he has no funds. What can he do? Well, he can go to a bank or a venture capital fund and borrow money based on the bank's or the fund's evaluation of his idea and its anticipated return on investment. He can then use this seed money to lease the building, purchase the machinery, and hire the people needed. He has created a concrete good or service out of nothing more than an idea. The asset of the new business, however, is balanced exactly by a liability: his debt to the bank. And at some point the debt has to be paid!

Similarly, we can conceive of our universe initially coming out of nothing by borrowing energy, according to Heisenberg's uncertainty principle. But nature is a merciless bookkeeper. The time allowed to repay the debt is very short. The more energy borrowed, the less time allowed. There would not be nearly enough time to allow our universe, let alone life, to evolve. But the universe used a clever trick to extend the time of its debt, the same trick a reckless government uses to extend or reduce repayment: inflation. An extremely fast expansion, far exceeding the speed of light, increased the size of the universe by untold billions in the first fraction of a second. Then the universe repaid, or at least pretended to repay, its debt, offsetting the positive of matter/energy by the negative of a gravity field.

Simplicity, Symmetry, and Beauty
gut and toe

We admire the beauty of the flower, the elegant simplicity of the crystal, the motion of the planets around the sun. In many ways, nature seems to indicate to us a basic symmetry and simplicity. From Archimedes to Newton to Einstein, physicists have tried to reduce the complexity of the observed world to an underlying set of basic laws and symmetries that govern it. When Mendeleyev discovered the symmetry of the periodic table, it allowed him to order the seemingly random proliferation of elements and go on to predict the existence of others that had not yet been discovered. Later, Niels Bohr and his colleagues were able to explain the 90 or so elements in terms of three basic subatomic particles: protons, neutrons, and electrons.

Unfortunately, further research has not continued to simplify the picture. To the contrary, analyzing the known subatomic particles has revealed a cornucopia of new ones. This brings up two very basic, very important questions. First, will we ever be able to explain the cosmos with one fundamental theory? I think the answer here is a qualified *yes*. Physicists are working very hard at what they call TOE, the Theory of Everything. They have made impressive progress explaining most of the basic forces of nature through the Grand Unified Theory (GUT), which unites the electromagnetic, weak, and strong nuclear forces into a single model. TOE is just an extension of GUT that attempts to incorporate the remaining force, gravity.

The second question is: If TOE is ever achieved, will it consist of a set of simple, elegant rules and equations with no arbitrary values or assumptions, capable of explaining the cosmos in all its complexity? Here my hunch is *no*. Rather, I believe we will always have to accept the existence of many seemingly *arbitrary* numbers and relationships. Even before one enters the realm of the physicist one sees some irregularities in this world of many symmetries. Relationships in nature show many seemingly arbitrary quirks and it is likely that the most basic laws and numbers will as well. If this were not so, it would imply that we are part of the one and only simple, basic universe. The quirks and arbitrariness we observe force us to the conclusion that ours is not the only universe. The reality that continues to emerge shows a great deal of order, but it also shows a great deal of arbitrariness as well. Why? Because it *worked*. The arbitrariness of the cosmos reveals that it is the product of chance and necessity, of survival, not design.

OTHER LIFE IN OUR GALAXY?

From a human-interest perspective, however, the most interesting question is not astrophysical but astrobiological. How probable is it that there is other life of the level of ours in our particular galaxy?

Well, there are about 100 billion stars in it. Of those, maybe one or two percent have the right size and the right temperature. But how many of those have planetary systems? So far, over 100 large extrasolar planets have been detected rotating around other stars in our galaxy. An average of a dozen new planets are being discovered each year, and 25 new planets were found during one five-day period in June 2002. Massive Jupiter-sized planets have been detected around about five percent of the stars studied. And they have all been detected by various indirect means rather than direct telescopic observation, which means that the larger Jupiter-sized ones are being discovered rather than the Earth-sized ones that are more likely to support life. How many of these would contain a planet like our Earth, with liquid water and continents, and an atmosphere with the right amount of O_2 and CO_2? All we can say is that, given our present knowledge, the probability is very low, but not zero.

When we look at photographs of the nine planets in the solar system, our Earth stands out like the one beautiful, bright, blue and white marble. I find it unlikely that there are very many Earth-like planets in our galaxy, but out of a billion possible ones, there must be a few. Do any of those have life like what we see on Earth today, including a species with intelligence comparable to our own? I think the probability is quite low. They may have life like the Earth had 100 million years ago, or 500 million years ago, but hardly intelligent life. Why? Our planet has had intelligent life for only some 100,000 years. Our species has had science and technology for less than 1,000 years. During the current millennium, humans will probably send spacecraft to investigate planets orbiting other stars in our galaxy.

If we compare the 12 billion years our universe has existed to a time span of 12 hours, then a million years equates to 1,000th of an hour, which is 3.6 seconds, and a thousand years equates to 3.6 milliseconds.

No intelligent extraterrestrial life has visited us in the past. It is likely that we will be traveling in space within a few hundred years and might discover such advanced civilizations. If they should be as advanced as we are, it would be similar to a situation in which two or more racers, starting their race at midnight, would all be reaching the goal (i.e., the state of advanced civilization) 12 hours later within the same few thousandths of a second – a most unlikely situation. Therefore we can say with some confidence that if an advanced civilization does exist in our own Milky Way galaxy, it is more likely that we will discover it, than that it will discover us.

Isn't it equally improbable, however, that we would be the only one in a billion to do so? Not really. The genes that each of us inherited from our parents represent the survivors, the best out of several millions. It is only because of a long series of consecutive improbable events that we are here on Earth to cogitate about these matters and enjoy doing so.

7

Evolution

Humanity's Place in Nature

MORE AND MORE it has become clear that Darwin's theory of evolution by natural selection is one of the two basic laws that govern not only life on Earth, but the development of the cosmos as well. What I like to call the process of "survival of the survivable" allowed life on Earth first to emerge from the primordial brew of the elements, and then elaborate and develop into ever more complex, ever more sophisticated systems and forms, culminating in the ascendance of humanity.

The *guiding hand* of evolution is not a kind one, however. It does not create *perfect* beings and protect them. Instead it throws forth all sorts of things. The ones with minimal discrepancies survive; the discrepant disappear.

This same law also presided over the creation of the cosmos out of chaos. I believe that the universe, with all its stars, with the laws of physics that govern it in all its immensity, is simpler and more basic than life, and even more so when compared against the human genome and the human brain it created. If those two appear more and more to be natural consequences of the working of random phenomena and of survival of the fittest, why not the universe itself? Indeed, modern physics, applying quantum theory to the earliest stages of the Big Bang, not only allows, but predicts the creation of many universes out of *nothing*, of which only the most survivable manage to survive.

DARWIN'S LAW
Creative destruction

In popular language, *Darwinism* means *survival of the fittest*. This, however, is a simplification and does not give the whole story. Who builds this *fittest* organism in the first place? And if only the *fittest* are able to survive, it must mean that an appalling number of the *less fit* are destroyed and their lines eliminated.

Darwin's law is best grasped as a process of creative destruction. The first, positive, creative aspect is the appearance of something, usually something more or less complex, often something that is in some way new or different. The second, negative aspect is the destruction of the many somethings usually described as *less fit*, but I believe it is more precise to term them *less survivable*.

Let's examine this process in more detail. First, let us look at the positive aspect, the creation of something different. When you roll a pair of dice, the odds are that you will get a number different from the one you had on the previous toss. That is the most simplistic meaning of something *new*.

Now consider the process physicists call *Brownian motion*. Look at a tiny particle suspended in a liquid, such as an oil spot in a pool of water. A second later it will be in a new, different location. In which direction will it move: up or down, right or left? By a very small distance or somewhat larger one? We don't know in advance. We will never know and never be able to know, because a basic law of nature forbids this. What we are witnessing is absolutely random, absolutely unpredictable motion – the creation of a new and different state purely through the operation of chance processes.

THE CREATIVE ASPECT
Mutation

In biology, a random change in the arrangement of one nucleotide at a specific location in the DNA of an organism is termed a *mutation*. Mutations may be due to cosmic radiation, attack by free radicals, or a mistake in the copying process during mitosis. Like Brownian motion, these mutations are random, totally unpredictable. The resulting mutant offspring (assuming it manages to be born) will be something new and different. The first, creative part of the evolutionary process has taken place.

Unfortunately, such innovations are generally detrimental to the individual and reduce its chance of survival. By far, most mutations are deleterious. The nondetrimental mutations are simply neutral. They neither help nor hinder the organism in its trials of life.

Then there are mutations that are *tolerable*. They affect the size of the body, the length of the arms or legs, the color of the eyes. Often they will cause a visible effect only when combined with other such mutations.

How about good mutations that provide the individual with a clear-cut advantage? I think we can say that these are almost nonexistent under steady-state conditions. A population has normally reached an optimal state in balance with its surroundings. It has reached an adaptive peak. Mutations will not make the population more fit, but they will create new alleles that will increase genetic diversity. It is like walking around the top of a mountain. No matter in which direction a person heads, he eventually ends up going down. The best he can do is to follow a flat path for a short distance. This is what neutral mutations do.

If the environment suddenly changes, however, the odds for survival change as well. A quick response by some members of the population in changing parts of their bodies through mutations (a longer coat, shorter claws, or sharper teeth, for example) would now be beneficial. But since a beneficial mutation means relying on a favorable roll of random dice, it would almost certainly come too late.

Life detests mutations. DNA molecules are tied through strong chemical bonds, and there are several mechanisms to correct any transcription errors. The one valuable function mutations can perform is to introduce and maintain diversity within a population, upon which selection can later operate when conditions change. Mutation provides a method by which a species can diversify its genetic portfolio in order to increase its odds of future survival.

Over a period of a hundred thousand years there may be quite a few *tolerable* mutations and existing genes will potentially have new alleles. Within a relatively short time, any such genetic change will be diffused through the entire population, often as a recessively transmitted feature. We now have a diverse population with thousands of genetically transmitted features, randomly distributed through its members.

The Creative Aspect
Sex

Can mutation alone possibly explain the grandeur of life we see around us and the diversity from which nature selects the fittest? Considering that most mutations are deleterious, most of the remainder are neutral, and only a very, very few are advantageous, it seems very unlikely. I believe that the answer lies in sexual reproduction. You often hear that sex is just a means of "rejuvenating the species" or "invigorating the next generation." Well, there are many species that reproduce asexually. Some of them are quite successful and hardy, as you know if you have ever tried to rid your lawn of dandelions.

Sexual reproduction is an extremely difficult, extremely complicated process. Most people, including many biologists, consider the creation of the first living cell to have been the critical, decisive step in the development of life on Earth. I disagree. I believe that this event was quite easy compared to the achievement of sexual reproduction. It probably took a few tens of millions of years to create the first primitive life, the first reproducing clump of protoplasm, while the evidence now suggests that it took three billion years before any organism succeeded in reproducing sexually. Only when that milestone was reached was evolution able to proceed by leaps and bounds to create the higher plants and animals. I believe that it was the advent of sexual reproduction that allowed the sudden (in evolutionary terms) appearance of the vast diversity of new life forms that is called the *Cambrian explosion.*

The reproduction of a living cell through simple division is no simple matter. First the chromosomes have to split, then rearrange themselves into two sets, each one properly receiving the thousands of parental genes. This procedure made life itself possible – and further evolution inevitable.

Sexual reproduction is far more complex. Here the cells have to perform an extraordinary reproductive process. First, the two sets of chromosomes have to be separated, with each set ending up in a new cell. Then each of these must find another cell that has performed the same procedure and fuse with it. Finally, the new cell formed from the two different sets of chromosomes must switch back to the process of normal cell division so the organism can develop. At first glance, it would seem to make successful reproduction so unlikely as to jeopardize the survival of the species.

The parental organisms often have to expose themselves to great danger in order to mate. Flying insects must climb into the evening sun in full view of rapacious birds. The hoofed animals of the plains must place themselves at the mercy of carnivores. Perhaps this is why it took nature three billion years to adopt such a procedure. Nature would hardly expose its creatures to such uncertainties if sexual reproduction were not a matter of the utmost importance.

Once this precarious process of sexual reproduction had been established, however, genetic diversity, and therefore the ability of a species to adapt to new environmental conditions or new ecological niches, could expand exponentially. Each offspring, rather than being a simple clone of its parent, would have two parents, four grandparents, eight great grandparents, a thousand ancestors after ten generations, and a million ancestors after 20 generations. In a population of a million individuals, everyone has a million times greater chance to inherit an advantageous mutation than it would have in a similar population where sexual reproduction did not exist. These individuals would, of course, inherit only the good mutations, since the bad ones would never survive the 20 generations. With such diversity to work with, evolution was able to proceed a thousand to a million times faster. Astonishing new opportunities then opened up for life on Earth. One of them would eventually lead to a large-brained, bipedal, tool-making primate: us.

NATURAL SELECTION
The destructive aspect

Creative life always brings forth many more individuals than the steady state can support. The death of the surplus individuals before they can reproduce – by predators, disease, accidents, or starvation when the population exceeds its food supply – is an unavoidable consequence. Only a minority survive long enough to reproduce. Who are these *fortunate* few? The common appellation of *the fittest* is an oversimplification. Luck plays a big part in determining who survives and who does not. Under steady-state conditions, it is mostly those who, by pure chance, have inherited less-favorable genetic traits, those at the extreme ends of the bell curve distribution, who are eliminated. This keeps the bell curve centered at a steady point and prevents it from enlarging excessively.

Evolution does not occur without great hardship. When conditions change, perhaps because of random factors, the odds for survival change as well. Mutations need not occur at this point. Earlier mutations have already supplied the population with an underlying diversity, which may partly reside in recessive characteristics that would show up in only a very few individuals. Under the new living conditions, some of these characteristics may turn out to be favorable and become prevalent in the population. This can happen quite fast without having to wait for new mutations to occur.

Take an honest look at our world, with all its blind cruelty, with its ignorance, diseases, wars, and hatreds, where wolves and lions can survive and feed their young only by tearing apart bright-eyed, gentle deer and gazelles. Does that look like the work of some benevolent, supremely intelligent, and omnipotent Creator, or the result of random, purposeless forces? As Darwin guessed over 140 years ago, it is a contest among the survivors in which the reward is survival.

A universe built by random forces out of chaos? Yes. Today's programmers have simulated this process using computers, creating objects of ever-increasing complexity, beauty, and regularity, by simply allowing a few parameters to take a random walk.

DOES EVOLUTION EQUAL PROGRESS?

Progress means movement, but it means much more. It means movement in a forward direction. You make progress on a trip when you keep on moving forward; if you turn around and go back, you are no longer progressing. That begs the question: What does *forward* mean? Does it mean a movement or transition from worse to better, from smaller to bigger, from weaker to mightier? Or does it mean movement toward some more desirable, more pleasant condition? Or does *forward* mean motion from the simple to the complex, or from the crude to the sophisticated?

When we compare our lives today to those of a farmer or an artisan in Europe 150 or 200 years ago, which life is more pleasant? If you compare today's stress-filled life of working eight or more hours a day on a job you find boring for a boss you dislike, only to go home to a world the media tells you is filled with crime, drugs, and suicide, you probably believe the farmer or artisan had it better. You may feel the same way if you compare the way we live in the United States or Europe with the indigenous peoples in South America or Indonesia, who lead (or used to lead) quiet lives governed by the old rules of the tribe, and, we are often told, have little crime, war, or divorce. We must ask: Has there been any progress from then to now?

But we should also turn the question around and ask: Does progress mean that things have to get better? Maybe not! From our viewpoint – perhaps from any viewpoint – humankind certainly progressed as we increased in intelligence; created culture, art, and science; and became undisputed masters of creation. On the other hand, are we happier spending eight hours in an office and two more hours driving our cars in logjams of traffic? Are we happier than a deer roaming freely through fields and forests? It would not appear so. Progress can hardly be seen as a movement toward increased happiness.

While there is little or no evidence for movement toward increasing happiness and satisfaction, there is very clear evidence in the evolution of life on Earth of progress along certain dimensions. Compare a primitive worm to a fish, then the fish to a bear, and finally the bear to a human. The bear may not be happier than the fish, nor the fish happier than the worm, but there is progress in the sense that the fish can *eat* the worm, the bear can eat the fish, and the human can hunt down the bear, skin it, and eat it. Alternatively, the human may keep the bear caged in a zoo, or maintain it in its natural environment by setting aside national parks. So, at least one definition of progress is increased power. This need not always be the case, however. A crocodile may eat a gazelle; a tiger may eat a human occasionally; and microbes can do them all in.

There is another characteristic that runs through all these examples, and that is complexity or sophistication. A fish is a more complex organism than a worm. It has powerful muscles, well-developed eyes, a central nervous system, and a brain. A warm-blooded bear, with its large, highly-developed brain and the ability to care for its young, is certainly a more behaviorally sophisticated organism than a fish – but then, the shark has survived for tens of millions of years, virtually unchanged. Unless the world's oceans should dry up, the shark has a chance of survival that is as good as or better than that of the bear, whose habitat humans keep destroying. This will remain true until we humans pollute the oceans as much as we already have polluted the land.

If we restrict our definition of *progress* to "an increase in complexity and sophistication," and do not expand it to include "a greater probability of survival," our brain power, our minds, our art, and our science all show that we are the most cognitively advanced, progressive form of life on Earth.

Of course, one could always examine some other characteristic, such as the sense of vision or smell, or the ability to run or swim quickly or fly. On those measures, humanity is hardly at the top of the scale. But our increased intelligence and technology have given us the ability to build machines to accomplish the same end results for us. It has even allowed us to build computers to increase our information-processing capability yet further. And that is progress.

As Darwin pointed out, there is clear anatomical evidence for the increasing complexity of the nervous system, especially the brain, among living animals. And while there were no human fossils yet found when Darwin wrote *The Origin of Species*, over a hundred years of anthropological research has since clearly established the progression in brain size from *Australopithecus* to *Homo erectus* to *Homo sapiens* along the lines that he predicted. We know that this increasing neurological complexity allows greater behavioral complexity.

Increased cognitive complexity (i.e., greater intelligence) generally places life forms higher on the food chain than less-complex, earlier forms.

If we agree on defining *progress* as "increased complexity," we must then conclude that the emerging global, technological society, in spite of its many problems, represents a higher stage of progress than any culture that has existed anywhere in the world at any other time. The question yet to be answered is whether we will use our vastly increased capabilities to solve our problems or only to worsen them.

8

Religion, Ethics, and Political Philosophy

OUR SPECIES is unique. We have sophisticated minds that cause us to worry about our future, to have a view of the universe, and to ask questions about our role in it. We don't just live hour to hour, day to day, with the only goals being to find food and evade predators. We need something more, something higher. Our minds have evolved to search for and construct some sense of *meaning* for our existence. This quest for meaning is the basis of our religious sentiment as well as our attachment to our tribe, our people, and our nation. At the highest level, it provides the root from which our pursuits of beauty and truth in the arts, the humanities, and science have grown.

When the Judeo-Christian ethos lost its grip on the Western worldview, it was replaced by Marxism and Freudianism. Long-standing moral precepts began to crumble and a slow but deep-reaching transformation began. A new philosophy of right and wrong was preached by the school system, academia, the media, and government. Seared into impressionable teenage minds by the powerful force of social acceptability, this philosophy bore such fruits as the sexual revolution, the drug culture, the crisis in confidence in government, and the decline of trust throughout society. The amalgam of Freudianism and Marxism eventually elevated these formerly negative and destructive tendencies into positive virtues.

Then, in the late 20th century, Marxism tumbled down with the Berlin Wall, and Freudianism crumbled before the weight of evidence from the hard sciences of behavior genetics and neurophysiology, leaving Marxism and Freudianism as little more than literary exercises. So, what is left? For some, a return to old-time religion. For far too many others, nothing but the quick fixes induced by promiscuous sex, mind-altering drugs, and conspicuous credit-card consumption.

I believe the Darwinian worldview, rightly understood, offers a solid alternative. But in far too many minds – and some very good and very decent minds – there is an unfair guilt by association with the excesses of the early eugenics movement and Hitler's genocide.

Politics must be built on some scientific or ethical basis. Otherwise, democracy becomes a mere popularity contest allowing politicians to get into office by promising the biggest tax breaks or the most government benefits. The only other alternative, which is even worse, is the brutal exercise of raw power.

THE LIBERAL LEFT

Today in philosophy, politics, and science there are two opposing camps. On one side are the Liberal Left; on the other, the Conservative Right. The Far Left denounce the Right as neo-Nazis; the Far Right retaliate in kind by calling the Left neo-Communists. Moving beyond such name-calling, what are the scientific and the ethical assumptions on which the two political philosophies rest? What are their similarities and their differences? The defining characteristic of the Liberal Left is that they are egalitarians. For them, it is an article of faith that all humans are equal at birth. Any differences that show up later in life – between individuals, sexes, races, or nations – are in no way the result of genes but of differences in social and economic conditions, education, or upbringing. In their worldview, there is no such thing as a basic human nature. Rather, they believe that our minds are infinitely malleable, so society creates human nature.

In the Soviet Union the nurture-over-nature theory reached an extreme when Stalin promoted the career of the pseudo-scientist Lysenko, who obediently performed experiments that supposedly *proved* that genes are so flexible they can be molded by their environment, and that these effects were passed on to the next generation. Lysenko's nonsense about the inheritance of acquired characteristics was elevated to a Stalinist dogma that all good communists had to believe. It then became the job of the party to create the ideal society of citizens who slavishly obey the party – and the party, of course, obeyed its leader.

While no one today seriously believes in the inheritance of acquired characteristics, perhaps as many as 80 percent of the academicians in the United States today, and even more in the humanitarian disciplines, adhere to some weaker form of the egalitarian dogma and the *tabula rasa* theory of the human mind. Ask most teachers, professors, politicians, or even many ministers about race and sex differences in mental abilities and aptitudes, or performance in various types of jobs or interests, and they will insist that whatever differences you see, or think you see, have nothing to do with the genes. Why? Because they assume that all humans are created equal, that mind and body are separate, and that *genetics is only skin deep*. Since they assume that there is no such thing as human nature or biological differences, whatever differences we see must be due to poverty, sexism, racism, dysfunctional families, and, of course, too little spending on education and social services. For if they deny the existence of human nature, they must necessarily accept the omnipotence of educational and governmental intervention in its place. The plain fact that 40 years of Great Society programs have proven counterproductive, even for those they were meant to help (though not necessarily for those who administer them), and that even the best early-intervention programs like Head Start have produced little or no lasting gains in IQ does not trouble them in the least. Their position appears to be: "Don't bother me with facts, since I know better."

It is amazing to me how stubborn and impervious to science some people can be. I sometimes wonder whether all of them really believe this or just pretend to in order to fit in with the group. I mean no insult by these statements. I simply want to show how the Liberal Left worldview is as much a declaration of faith, immune to empirical refutation, as the worldview of the Religious Right that it takes such delight in ridiculing.

THE RELIGIOUS RIGHT

What about the opponents of the Left, the Conservative Right? One of its wings, the Religious Right, is as uninterested in looking at facts as is its opposite number on the Far Left. While few of the Religious Right still believe the Earth is flat, they actively oppose the teaching of evolution in our schools unless it is presented alongside some disguised form of biblical creation. They see their religious commandments as ethical guard rails that keep their children from falling into the abyss of moral relativism. And their faith in God gives them the courage to oppose the attempts by the Left to make government into a god. The Religious Right oppose governmental intervention – except when it comes to sexual and reproductive behavior. Here they not only reject the "if it feels good, do it" philosophy of the Left, but also equate abortion with genocide and oppose birth control and family planning, even if such practices would truly help those least able to bring up children.

THE PROBLEM-MAKERS

Having described the clash of political philosophies, we must now examine the sectors of our society that currently frame the debate:

The Academics and the Intelligentsia

Professors are notorious for having one-track minds. Engrossed in their particular subject matter and cloistered in their ivory towers, they can be surprisingly naive about other fields or even life in general. Perhaps that is part of the reason communism, socialism – and, for that matter, fascism and Nazism – have had strong adherents among the ranks of academia and the intelligentsia. Often from rich and "good" families and the products of private schools, many academics lack a deeper understanding of the real world.

Cervantes' Don Quixote and Voltaire's Dr. Pangloss provided portraits of this mentality, but writers of the 17th and 18th centuries could not have foreseen the genocidal extreme to which it could go in our own time. With their minds wide open to utopian but simplistic slogans about either the equality or the inequality of all humans, nations, and races, these academics and intelligentsia are the intellectual descendants of the ancient priests who gave us religion, not of the craftsmen who gave us science.

Sadly, these are the very individuals into whose hands our society increasingly entrusts the young and impressionable minds of our children, cutting them loose from the restraining influence of their parents' practical wisdom and the accumulated common sense of past generations.

The Politicians

Practical politicians (as opposed to revolutionaries) are, for the most part, intelligent and highly articulate individuals. But all too often they are people of action, with neither time for nor interest in deep thinking. A certain amount of pragmatism is desirable to protect society from dictators like Stalin or Hitler who want to remake the world in their own image. But too much pragmatism can result in an intellectual cowardice that can be bullied into submission. A great politician must be able to discern the difference between those causes that are worth fighting for and those that are not.

The Media

For better or for worse, the media have become the most powerful force in modern democratic nations. They determine which issues are discussed and they have the ability to form public opinion. No group has greater power to provide society at large with the best knowledge in an understandable form. But they have the same power to provide biased, misleading information.

Do they really believe in so many demonstrably false tenets of the egalitarian dogma? I don't think so. For the most part, they are too intelligent for that. Some have a literary or journalistic background and so are not equipped to deal with statistics and science. But others are so equipped, and they write very clearly about astronomy, physics, and biology, but only rarely about the science of human behavior and human differences. Far too many individuals are fearful of losing their jobs, their television ratings, or their book sales. Who wants to lose his job in disgrace? Instead they live by the motto: "Happy is he who can forget about that which cannot be changed anyway." If humankind is to survive, however, we must replace this with the motto: "There can never be any shame in seeking, knowing, or telling the truth."

THE SCIENTIFIC RIGHT

There is also a less extreme form of conservatism that I shall call the Scientific Right. What are their beliefs and how do they contrast with those of the Liberal Left and the Religious Right?

First, they deny the power of even the most powerful state to form society in its own image. In short, they believe in a basic underlying human nature. And they believe that culture is at least as much the result of human nature as human nature is the result of culture. The Religious Right also accepts the reality of human nature – they just attribute it to God rather than Darwinian evolution.

For the Left, poverty and racism cause the low IQ of some segments of society. For the Scientific Right, the evidence shows that, to a significant degree, low IQ causes poverty and low motivation, and both of these reflect the complex interaction of *nature × nurture* described earlier. It is a question of cause and effect. For the Left, education will be the salvation of society. For the Religious Right, all the answers are in the Bible. For the Scientific Right, things will never be that simple or that easy.

The Scientific Right believes we must take account of both nature and nurture, heredity and environment. Education is essential, but it can do only so much. A worthy challenge for our society is to find a compassionate means of shifting the bell curve distribution for intelligence and character in the positive direction that also respects the constitutional and human rights of all its members. But how? What brought the early eugenics movement into disrepute was its attempts at easy, simplistic solutions. And like the Far Left, it called for massive governmental action.

Both the Right and the Left were seduced by the same utopian desire for a quick, simple solution to problems with deep, almost intractable roots. In a democracy the government cannot control its citizens. It cannot tell them how to reproduce. Everyone should be free to do what he or she likes, but should not then expect society to bear the costs of his or her self-destructive behavior. Our society could stop providing monetary incentives for having more children to those least capable of providing their children with a good life. It could provide people with the information and the materials to practice birth control and family planning voluntarily. And it could provide greater child care and a better educational system for those who are able to bring up children and are interested in doing so.

WHERE DO I STAND?

So, where do I stand? Am I with the Liberal Left or the Conservative Right? I am neither! My position is the one I have described as the Scientific Right. When I look at the evidence, it shows me that what the Liberal Left have done has been so counterproductive that more of the same would be disastrous.

I agree with the Conservative Right that in many, maybe most, cases, the best thing that government can do is to get out of the way. Governmental bureaucracy is placing an ever-increasing burden on small businesses, which create the new technologies and new jobs, and provide the expanding opportunities we so desperately need. And government is also becoming increasingly and annoyingly intrusive in our private and family lives.

Unlike the Conservative Right, however, I think that government should get out of the way also in the area of reproductive technology. It should foster the development of biotechnology, cloning, and stem cell research. Both in the United States and especially in the Third World, governments should not outlaw abortion and birth control, nor force them upon people. The best way government can promote *family values* is by reducing the total tax burden on the middle class and by providing scholarships to qualified students so that children do not become a luxury affordable only by the very affluent or a burden dumped on society by the destitute and self-indulgent.

And unlike the Conservative Right, I believe that there are areas in which government must play a vital role. It is hard to tell which of these will have greatest impact, but they will all certainly play a decisive role in the long-range future of humanity. They are:

- the exploration of space
- the development of biotechnology
- the preservation of our planet's biodiversity
- the unshackled examination of the nature/nurture question as it pertains both to individuals and to groups, and its implications for the genetic future of humankind
- the preservation of our cultural and genetic diversity

If we ignore these areas, we will be gambling humanity's survival on the false hope that the problems we will face in the future will not be serious enough to warrant any inconvenience in the present.

9

Our Modern Dilemma

Where Does Humanity Go from Here?

My Concerns

I am worried, very much worried, about the future of our human race on this planet. Students of evolution and of animal behavior well know that any species that does not have to fight for survival, that has no predators and can find food without effort, will degenerate in the course of time. Northern Indians and Eskimos can tell stories and legends that show how wolves play an important role in keeping reindeer herds healthy and strong, because they more readily catch the sickly and weak, and leave the healthy and strong to reproduce the race.

Up until some 150 years ago, humanity lived under similar conditions. Couples had large families, but not all children survived. Those with congenital defects or those not mentally strong enough to overcome the many hardships and diseases of those days often died before maturity, and even those who survived were less likely to find a mate and reproduce. On the other hand, the more physically and mentally talented individuals had a better chance to find a mate and could afford a larger family. This situation may not have prevailed all the time and everywhere, but certainly played an important role in keeping the human race healthy, and even may have eventually led to improving the human genome somewhat. However, a high price had to be paid: Humans were subject to the tough and often cruel laws of nature.

Today things are quite different, especially in the advanced countries. Food is abundant and many dangerous diseases have been eradicated or can readily be treated. Thanks to our great wealth, we are able to support those unable to support themselves. Through drugs and medical assistance, children with both mental and physical genetic defects are often kept alive to reproductive age. It is quite obvious: Our welfare states, with the best intentions, have turned Darwin's inexorable law right on its head. No species in such conditions can long survive.

Some symptoms of the slow mental and physical genetic deterioration may already be showing. In spite of the great effort our country expends to give the best possible education to all its citizens, American high school graduates score near last on the list of advanced countries. This could be due to the fact that our students do not attach much importance to those tests or maybe that our educational system rates so low – it's difficult to tell. However, if this disturbing situation is due to a slow downward trend in the aptitude level of the American population, it is a quite worrisome signal.

Though controversial and rejected by the Liberal Left, there is a considerable body of work that clearly establishes the connections between mentalities of individuals and groups, and their relative performances and successes in societies. *The Bell Curve*, for instance, by Richard Herrnstein and Charles Murray, is among the better-known works. In my view, these connections are relevant and worthy of further study without political-correctness and taboos obstructing such studies.

The painful shortage of highly competent people is already hurting u.s. industry and forces it to import many scientists, doctors, engineers, and highly skilled workers from other countries. These countries, in turn, need more competent people themselves and resent the brain drain we cause.

All these observations seem to confirm what Darwin's theory would predict: a sheltered group tends to degenerate. This degeneration is not limited to the advanced countries. In Third World countries, people's lives have also been much changed under European and American influence and involvement. The reduced procreation of highly educated individuals is not limited to the West.

The same is observed in well-to-do groups in all parts of the world.

There is no doubt that some scientists may strongly disagree with my pessimistic views. The facts mentioned above could be interpreted in different ways. Also, the time period involved is extremely short in relation to the time it took nature to develop *Homo sapiens*. On the other hand, destroying a work of art that was slowly built under great pains is always much easier and much faster than creating it. In my view the situation is very critical and I view it with considerable concern. I want to be clear that I mean to say no more than that it should be studied. Unfortunately, few researchers like to deal with an unpleasant situation that most people would rather ignore. If a great potential danger appears to be lurking on the horizon, we should not brush it off and stick our heads in the sand. We should rather confront it squarely and courageously.

As a typical example, let us look at today's environmental concerns. If you had told an industrialist a hundred years ago that the emissions from his plant could pollute rivers, lakes, and even part of the ocean, that the emissions from his power plant could alter the Earth's climate, he would have scoffed at these fears. He would have felt that the relatively minute emissions from his plant could not possibly affect the vastness of the oceans or influence the whole enormous mass of the Earth's atmosphere, and that your statement was ridiculous. He would have contended that nature emits much more pollutants through its volcanoes, for instance, and he would have stressed the fact that nature is so immense and so much more powerful than we insignificant humans that we could hardly affect its workings.

Well, today we humans are overpowering nature and we are greatly affecting our natural environment. This is becoming a great concern to many people on this planet. The environmentalists have created a powerful movement. We now realize how unique our planet is in its greatness, beauty, and diversity. We know that we have to conserve carefully what nature has built because whatever species become extinct, whatever we destroy, can never be replaced and is gone forever.

I suspect that 20 or 50 years from now people may finally become aware of the fact that there is another, even greater, immensely more complex and more sophisticated work of art, the most sublime that nature has ever created. That is the human mind in its most noble form. We are now in the process of slowly and steadily downgrading our internal environment – the human genome. It too is a delicate creation that needs care and protection, and that should be conserved for posterity without degrading its exquisite design. If we let it deteriorate beyond repair, it will be gone, and with it our cultural heritage. We will never be able to bring it back because its complexity goes well beyond anything the human mind could ever conceive.

HUMAN DIVERSITY

One of the important goals of the environmental movement is to maintain the great diversity nature has created. Considerable efforts are applied today to prevent the loss of this diversity. However, important changes are now taking place in our internal environment that will greatly affect the future of humankind and are going unnoticed. Not only are we witnessing the fast decrease in the percentage of the more competent individuals because of a lower rate in procreation, but also we are witnessing the even faster decrease in whole groups of people, in entire nations. This will severely affect the diversity now existing in the human genome that should be conserved. The rate of procreation in most European countries is now so low that, if not changed drastically, will bring about practical extinction in some 15 to 20 generations. In Germany, for instance, only one in a thousand Germans will have survived after as few as 15 generations. Estonia, a nation with a very decent, hard-working population of only one million people with a very distinct genetic and linguistic origin, is shrinking almost as fast. This is a trend that is likely to extend to other parts and peoples of the world as they advance toward prosperity and the improved status of women.

Fortuitous arrangements of the three billion nucleotides that make up a special human genome have brought forth the great geniuses, the great statesmen, and the great creators of our art and our literature. However, this alone could never create a civilized nation. It also requires an infrastructure of working phones, a dependable supply of electric power, a well-maintained network of highways, water, and sewage systems. All this requires crews of hard-working, dedicated and dependable workers. Such qualities reside in the human genome, but if this genome deteriorates, these qualities will become rare and motivated people will become harder to find.

Genes and Memes

Experts in genetics know that it is only the genome that a young individual inherits from his ancestors, but that is not the only thing that determines what kind of person he or she will become as an adult. Genes are required to provide a healthy, highly sophisticated base. However, they only form a skeleton on which the meat still has to be attached. The fact is, genes and *memes* (a set of ideas and values that regulate behavior and actions of groups) are both needed. A solid cultural input has to be provided through parental upbringing, education in school, and, most effectively, the examples set by peers. However, if the skeleton has deteriorated, there will be nothing substantial on which to attach the meat, and neither a good upbringing nor extensive schooling will take hold. Without a highly selected, highly sophisticated genetic base, culture cannot survive and a civilized society will soon disappear.

In recent years genetic science and genetic engineering have made enormous strides. Couldn't we expect that this technology will someday be able to repair any damage that may have been inflicted on the human genome? To answer this question, we need to take a look at what the new science of genetics can and what it cannot do.

THE HUMAN GENOME

If a treasured painting stored in a museum shows a little scratch or a tiny hole, an art lover may consider it a catastrophe, but the damage can easily be repaired. However, if one of the most admired paintings is lost, all the modern painters in the world will not be able to replace it. The loss to the world of art would be great, even though a number of great paintings would still exist, as would a much larger number of other paintings.

The situation is quite similar with regard to the human genome. Reverting to the above example, we would say: If the most valuable human genome was lost, all the geneticists in the world could not replace it. In the human realm, however, the situation could be much worse since not only a few great paintings are lost, but many other valuable paintings are slowly deteriorating.

Congenital diseases are being transmitted at an increasing rate. These diseases are normally caused by a mutation in just one or two of the three billion nucleotides that form the genome.

Genetic medicine has developed a procedure by which the affected gene can be replaced by a healthy one. It is not a simple or easy procedure. The healthy gene first has to be introduced in a virus, which then can penetrate the cell membrane and disgorge all its genes into the cell. Sometimes by chance the cell nucleus absorbs the good gene and introduces it into the correct chromosome to replace the faulty gene. The rest of the virus' genes, however, may create havoc in their host. This makes the procedure so uncertain and so hazardous that after a decade of tests and efforts, some medical specialists recommend abandonment of this technique altogether. Even if it could eventually be greatly improved, such genetic operation will amount to only the equivalent of repairing the little scratch or tiny hole in the valuable painting.

Furthermore, this genetic procedure would help only one individual. The faulty gene would still reside in his reproductive cells and be transmitted to his offspring. In order to make the repair permanent, germline engineering is required. This would involve replacing the faulty gene in a fertilized egg, so that all the cells, including the reproductive cells of the future individual, would profit and all his descendants would be free of the defect. However, such repair work has never been done and it is uncertain whether it will be possible or even desirable.

At this point, the reader may ask: What about our genetically modified crops? Aren't they an indication that permanent modifications of a species' genes are practically possible? The problem here is that the methods used are more akin to breeding than to true genetic engineering and people would not take kindly to a government that tries to breed them.

It should also be noted that in all the genetic work accomplished so far, scientists have used genes or parts of chromosomes that nature had developed over millions of years of trials. Nothing really new has been artificially created. It would be an immense task to design from scratch a complete gene with its 10,000 or more nucleotides arranged in proper sequence and with the proteins that control its expression. Will it be possible to do this in the future?

It is always a risky undertaking to state that a certain thing is impossible and can never be done. There is a saying that the person who says something cannot be done is often interrupted by someone who is doing it. So, let us assume that someday our scientists will understand the function of each of the 30,000 genes of the human genome, as well as their more than 100,000 alleles, and that they will be able to recreate those genes that have been lost forever in a deteriorating society by proper arrangement of their 10,000 nucleotides.

If this should someday become possible, it would still require the introduction of such a set of artificial chromosomes into an egg that has been surgically removed from a woman, then the reintroduction of this egg into the womb of a woman who would then give birth to a *superhuman* baby. This would be a rather difficult and expensive operation. Only a very small minority of the people then populating the Earth would be willing and able to undergo such a procedure. This would create a minority class of superhumans while the majority of humanity would be left to sink ever deeper into poverty and decay – not a desirable future.

There must be some better way to maintain the human genome for posterity.

Misguided Eugenics

More than 100 years ago, after Darwin had published his famous works, some scientists and political leaders realized that humanity might be engaged on a dangerous path, a path that was hardly in accordance with Darwin's teachings. This gave birth to the misguided eugenic movement, which was subsequently abused. Most great minds of those days were strong advocates for some kind of action to prevent humanity from degenerating. Theodore Roosevelt, George Bernard Shaw, and Winston Churchill were among them. Laws were enacted to sterilize people suffering from severe physical and mental defects that ran in families. Not just in Hitler's Germany, but also in the United States and in many European countries, such laws were legislated. Sterilization, however, was normally ordered only after it had been approved by a court of law and generally with the consent of the concerned people. Funds were proposed and payments were distributed to encourage intelligent couples to have more children. These actions were typical for a time of great optimism, when Western nations felt that any problem could be solved through easy solutions.

Today a less optimistic, more seasoned philosophy has taken hold in respect to social matters. It would be totally inconceivable to reintroduce such procedures, and no civilized country would accept them – and, of course, should not.

What, then, can be done to preserve humankind in a healthy state for the long-range future? At this point, I would say: "Not very much." Today's frame of mind still suffers from the holocaust of two awful World Wars and the remembrance of human experiments done under Stalin's and Hitler's reigns. People therefore oppose any social engineering of any sort ... and this may be just as well.

Matters of procreation are too important to ever be left in the hands of any government. No bureaucrat should have the right to tell people what to do in these matters.

In fact, governments supported by political and religious groups often seem intent to do what will best ensure the steady deterioration of the human genome and consequently the slow degeneration of the human race. For example, with best intent, governments support people at the lowest level of society, thus encouraging them to have more offspring, while middle class families are punished by the marital surtax and cannot easily afford to have more than two children because of the ever-rising cost of higher education.

In the developing world where life had seen little change over centuries, we have raised havoc through our intrusion and the introduction of our technical gadgets. Populations that were stable before, leading natural lives before we brought our technology, are now exploding in numbers, on the one hand, and being decimated by diseases like AIDS, on the other hand. Humanity is faced with some very critical problems today, all of its own making.

Whether we like it or not, the time has come when intelligent sociobiological action has become necessary.

For those who remember some 50 or 60 years ago, our Western world especially was faced with problems of similar magnitude concerning our natural environment. Our fast-expanding industry and our more numerous cars were poisoning the environment, and many species of plants and animals were disappearing at an increasing rate. This gave birth to the environmental movement, which has become a very strong presence in our society. It is not its goal to improve what nature has created, to breed bigger and better species of elephants or mountain gorillas; the goal is to prevent their extinction, which would cause an irreparable loss of diversity. The aim of the environmental movement is to *maintain* the great diversity that nature created before the advent of our civilization.

Similarly, as far as the human species on this planet is concerned, the goal should be the same. We should not try to breed a better race *à la* Hitler, but we should try to maintain what nature built and not let it deteriorate through dysgenics. We have to maintain the great diversity of human intellect and human abilities.

WHAT CAN BE DONE?

But how should we go about this? A complete change of our approach to life and society will be required. First of all, our government should stop its anti-Darwinian actions; it should no longer abet procreation by those who are not mentally competent to raise a family properly. In fact, neither government nor legislators should mix into matters of procreation. There should be no incentives, neither pro nor con. Matters of procreation should be entirely left up to the individuals. Any action in this field should be coming from the grass roots up, not from the government down. Every person has to be free to make his or her own decision. Most often a decision that is best for an individual will also be best for the future of humanity as a whole. The less the government mixes into social matters, the better it is for the total community.

Does this mean that we will have a Darwinian society? Not at all! We are a compassionate society. We are bound to care for the less endowed, for those who would be left indigent. Compassion for the less fortunate has to be part of any civilized society. But caring for those in the lower ranks of society does not mean that we should, through misplaced incentives, encourage individuals to have offspring who have no interest in children and who may end up neglecting them. In a civilized society, children deserve the right to grow up in a stable, healthy family. On the other hand, those parents who are part of the hard-working middle class, who are proud of their healthy offspring and duty-bound to care for them, should be able to give them proper education at a reasonable cost to whatever level they are capable of achieving.

Today people ready to procreate have many options available without resorting to genetic engineering. Some couples may decide for artificial insemination; some may want to use donated sperm and donated eggs; some may resort to test tube fertilization with selection and implantation of the healthiest embryo; and some may renounce procreation altogether. The majority will, of course, feel quite satisfied with their own genetic endowment and will keep creating new human beings without having to resort to any special method. Admittedly, some of the aforementioned procedures – except for the last one – are slow, expensive, and sometimes involve surgical intrusion. How could poor people who may benefit from it the most afford it? It should be expected that these things are bound to become simpler, cheaper, more predictable, and more routine as their use increases. Furthermore, insurance could be provided to support parents who judge that such procedures are required in the interest of their children. With a healthy population, with fewer physical and mental diseases – which, if unaddressed, are bound to become more prevalent and more expensive – the nation will over the years save many times the money spent to help those couples produce healthier offspring.

Dissemination of proper information is the key to achieving a well-functioning society. People who are correctly informed are generally more than willing to do the right thing: what is good for them and for the society they live in, what is good for the future of their country, and what will benefit their children and their children's children.

Are people well informed today? Certainly not! In fact, they are badly misinformed. Human differences and the importance of heredity and of the genes are taboo subjects. The preferred view is that all humans are created equal and that it is the environment that makes the differences.

It is impossible to understand the future and even more impossible to positively affect the future based on misguided information. We would not expect a scientist who believes in a flat Earth to guide a rocket to the moon.

In order to remedy the problems affecting humanity today, we will first have to allow the truth to be disseminated freely, and we will have to eliminate all the taboos that now hamper free research and the publication of facts that may be politically undesirable. Only the dissemination of the truth, the whole truth, and nothing but the truth will lead humanity into a brighter future.

10

The Foundations of a Good Society

THERE ARE two very basic, very elementary causes that determine the behavior, success, and wealth of any people: its culture and its genetic base. What makes a nation is its people, their intellectual ability, their values, their moral fiber, and their industriousness. And these are products of the interaction of their genes with their cultural environment.

Nature and nurture, that is, genes and early upbringing, largely determine the future direction of a person's life – whether he will be a scientist or a criminal, a successful professional or a failure. Surely there are other factors, too, such as being in the right (or wrong) place at the right (or wrong) time, family wealth and connections, and finally good or bad luck. Moving from one environment – say, from the former Soviet Union – to a totally different one, like that of the United States, can also affect an individual's future by opening new opportunities to express his or her abilities and talents. But all these factors are far less important than is generally thought. Personality and character, the product of nature interacting with nurture, are far more powerful.

The same is true also for groups, nations, and peoples. The characteristics of a given nation – its wealth, its success, its social stability or crime level, and its ability to contribute to the rest of humanity through its creativity in science, art, and technology – depend in equal parts on its genetic makeup and its culture, its traditions, history, and religion or ethical code. These latter elements were, of course, largely created through the influence of the former in complex interactions.

People, not geography, climate, or even natural resources, make a nation what it is. It is no accident that, for the most part, the wealthiest nations are those with the highest average intelligence, while the poorest nations have the lowest. Why? Certainly differences in human capital – the accumulated stores of knowledge, skills, and education – are very important. And many of these cultural traditions are so subtle and deeply ingrained that they can take generations to adjust to new conditions. But however politically incorrect or unpopular it may be, we must also be willing to examine the genetic basis of average group differences in intelligence and character, just as we do for individuals.

I am not saying that genes are everything! We have clear examples that show the effect that the form of government can have. Consider the former East and West Germany or North and South Korea. The people are genetically much the same, with maybe some minor differences. Perhaps immigration of the most enterprising individuals also played a part. But clearly 50 years of communist rule eroded the high work ethic of both the East Germans and the North Koreans who were unfortunate enough to fall under its control. Of course, it is always easier to destroy than to build up.

Ethnic diversity and homogeneity probably also play

a role in national achievement. In Estonia, a small, ethnically homogeneous country, it has been much easier to make the transition to a free-market democracy because all the citizens feel a sense of being one big, extended family. There is little sense of the resentment we have seen develop between the former East Germans and their Western relatives. But diversity can also add much-needed spice to a nation. Certainly the United States has benefited from the immigration of intelligent, hard-working, honest people from all over the globe. There is probably some optimal balance between a stifling homogeneity and a disruptive heterogeneity. Differences in birth rates can greatly amplify the latter effect, however, until the system swings completely out of control.

Is History Scientific?

Like psychology, the study of history today is at the stage where chemistry was in the Middle Ages: It is mostly the repetition of impressive-sounding, but scientifically meaningless incantations. We tend to place great importance on things like education, the economy, military power, and the form of government. But changes in government, economic booms and busts, and military victories and defeats are only short-term ripples in the life of nations. The river runs much deeper. Nations reflect their people, rather than vice versa.

The Marxist view of history as being totally guided by economic factors is very simplistic and primitive. The wealth and stability of nations are largely based on the intelligence, capabilities, and moral fiber of their individuals.

Golden Rules, Cardinal Virtues, and Mortal Sins

Most religions have some Golden Rule such as "do unto others as you would have them do unto you" or "the root of all suffering is desire." The Roman emperor and Stoic philosopher Marcus Aurelius listed wisdom, justice, temperance, and fortitude as his Four Cardinal Virtues, while the Medieval Church preached that greed, gluttony, lust, envy, sloth, wrath, and pride were the Seven Mortal Sins.

My Golden Rule is that we should seek the truth, the whole truth, and only the truth, no matter how unpopular, even if this truth disagrees with religious or politically correct beliefs. The only thing I cannot tolerate is intolerance.

The Traits That Build a Good Society

There is a set of basic abilities or qualities – call them *cardinal virtues*, if you like – that are necessary for the functioning of a modern, technological society. Any nation, group, people, or individual that lacks these qualities cannot fully participate in all that today's global, technological economy has to offer. Increasing any one of these qualities makes a society more prosperous and more humane – in short, a better place to live. Decreasing them starts the slide, even if ever so slowly, toward the abyss.

Intelligence

The first quality on the list is *intelligence*. Given the knowledge of his day, Marcus Aurelius was wise to place *wisdom* first on his list. The problem is that wisdom is subjective. As the Supreme Court justice said of pornography: "We can't define it, but we all know it when we see it." On the other hand, we can measure intelligence rather precisely. It is a valid measure that predicts success in school, work, and life in general for almost all individuals, regardless of religion, nationality, sex, or race, unless they were brought up in the most horrid of conditions.

Integrity

The second quality is *integrity*, by which I mean character, moral fiber, trustworthiness and dependability. A person with the highest intelligence but lacking in moral character can do a great deal to hurt society.

Drive

Great accomplishments also require a high level of *drive*, and here is where I find the Stoic philosophy wanting. The achievements of Western society have been based on its active interest in trying to understand nature so that we could harness its immense powers, not trying to reconcile ourselves to it. Nature will always be stronger.

Inhibition

Drive, however, must be balanced by the quality of *inhibition*, by which I mean a mechanism of internal, moral control. Great scientists, reformers, and business leaders possess above-average levels of drive – but so do tyrants, mass murderers, and psychopaths.

Broad, General Education

We must not overlook the value of a *broad, general education*. In our recent emphasis on technology, we have paid this quality too little attention and given it too little support. But without it, each succeeding generation will lose contact with where it came from and therefore have less and less understanding of where it is going.

A Sense of Humor

Finally, a *sense of humor* and the ability to entertain ourselves and others are important. This will be particularly true if we travel in space, and I am confident that we will someday meet the challenges and overcome the obstacles we certainly will encounter.

THE TRAITS THAT UNDERMINE A GOOD SOCIETY

We can get a list of modern mortal sins by looking at these qualities from the negative perspective, that is, how much danger they pose to the survival of our society. Here, however, I would list them in a slightly different order.

Low IQ

First on the list is a lack of general intelligence. Without a high overall IQ, modern technological society is impossible. The more complex our economy becomes, the greater its demands for cognitive ability. Individuals, groups, and nations at the low end of the bell curve find themselves falling further and further behind, left out, or dependent on the charity of others. And this can breed envy, resentment, and even hostility if they are also lacking in inhibition.

Impulsivity

The lack of inhibition and self-control moves up to the Number 2 position. At the individual level, lack of internal moral restraint results in sociopaths and psychopaths: the rapists, murderers, and serial killers. When found in persons holding positions of power, however, a lack of inhibition gives rise to genocidal dictators like Hitler or Stalin, whose victims are far more numerous than all the *everyday* criminals combined.

Corruption

The third most dysfunctional quality is a lack of integrity: lying, stealing, and cheating. These behaviors are destructive of any family and can lead a business, even one that provides a valuable product or service, into bankruptcy. The acceptance of widespread corruption keeps some countries from rising up in the world, even though the people of those countries possess a reasonably high level of intelligence.

Indolence

Fourth on the list of modern deadly sins is lack of a sufficient level of drive or achievement motivation. This causes individuals, families, and nations to languish in self-satisfied mediocrity.

Ignorance

Finally, ignorance, by which I mean a low level of general education, is by no means bliss. Rather, it strips us of any sense of history. Even the most intelligent society would not want to have to rediscover all the accumulated knowledge and culture of past generations.

THE EQUATION FOR A GOOD SOCIETY

Intelligence, integrity, drive, inhibition, and even educational level are the result of *nature* × *nurture*. We can increase or decrease these positive traits by changing either term in the equation, though it is easier and more politically acceptable to deal with the *nurture* side of the equation.

Sadly, in recent years the permissive philosophy of moral relativism that grew out of Freudianism, combined with the resentment preached by Marxism, has served to remove moral inhibition and reduce drive, and to replace them with a philosophy of "if it feels good, do it." It has also justified lying, stealing, and cheating, even at the highest levels of government and industry. Attempts to correct unacceptable behavior or provide much-needed guidance and discipline have been dismissed as "blaming the victim," and the words *racism* and *sexism* have degenerated into mere ritual terms of abuse or self-abuse.

THE CHALLENGES FOR OUR SOCIETY

If we are to survive, our society must first focus on gathering information. This requires a look at both the genetic and the environmental sources of human nature and human diversity. Only then can science inform the intelligentsia and the media so that they, in turn, can disseminate the information throughout society. Finally, any candidate for public office and any graduate of a college or university should be able to address the following questions intelligently:

- How are changes in birth rates, mortality rates, and reproductive technology affecting humanity's genetic base and the demand we place on the environment?
- What role are immigration and emigration, *brain gains* and *brain drains* playing in changing the demographic composition of the world?
- What role do genes and environment play in the traits and abilities that are needed in today's global, technological society?
- What goals, such as space exploration and travel, can inspire humanity and give us a sense of purpose for the new millennium?

Answering these questions is a long-term goal that will require not only a high level of intelligence, integrity, and drive, but also an openness to explore new ideas and a willingness to abandon old ones that have proven outdated or counterproductive.

Can humanity meet the challenges? In the short term I may have sounded somewhat pessimistic, but in the long term I am optimistic. Why? Because we will have to!

Any effective change must come from the bottom up, not from the top down. For that to happen, academia and the media must disseminate the truth, as best we know it at any given point in time, to the people. Only then will we be capable of making informed decisions and taking corrective actions critical to the survival of our species, our planet, and perhaps intelligent life itself.

My hope is that these reflections can help to break down the taboos that have restricted open inquiry into these controversial issues and that they provide a mental map with which we can begin to explore the questions that lie at the borderlands of our present knowledge of our cosmos and ourselves.

ABOUT WALTER KISTLER

A VISIONARY with the resources and discipline to drive his vision into reality is an individual who can make a difference in the future of the world. Such a visionary is Walter Kistler, a physicist and inventor who for years kept alive his vision of endowing a foundation focused on increasing and diffusing knowledge about the long-term future of humanity. This is the story of the unfolding of that vision.

Walter Kistler was born in Biel, Switzerland, in 1918, the third of three children born to Hermann Kistler, a lawyer, and Marguerite Jeanneret, a nurse. Even as a boy Walter was interested in rocketry and space mechanics – an interest that has continued into his 80s. He studied sciences at the University of Geneva and earned a Master's degree in physics from the Federal Institute of Technology in Zurich.

In 1944, at age 26, Walter went to work for the Swiss Locomotive and Machine Works, Winterthur, and subsequently spent several years as the head of its Instrumentation Lab. During this time, he pioneered a new measurement technology using Piezo-electric quartz crystals as the transduction element in accelerometers, load cells, and pressure gauges. What made this new technology possible was Walter's own invention of a charge amplifier that could handle the very high impedance signals obtained from such sensors. In 1983 he received the prestigious Albert F. Sperry Award from the Instrument Society of America (ISA) for these achievements.

In 1951 Walter moved to the United States, where he joined Bell Aerosystems, Buffalo, New York. At Bell, he invented and developed a pulse constraint servo-accelerometer that was later used in the guidance of the Agena space rocket. For this work, he received the 1968 Aerospace Pioneer Award from the American Institute of Aeronautics and Astronautics (AIAA), recognizing "his pioneering effort in the development of high-performance aerospace instrumentation."

Wishing to further pursue his work in quartz instrumentation, Walter founded Kistler Instrument Corporation in 1957. This company became a world leader in the development of quartz sensors. One of the major innovations under his supervision was the invention and development of the Piezotron, a semiconductor module that made a high-impedance quartz sensor to a low-impedance instrument. Several accelerometers of this type were used in the Apollo manned spaceflight project. Through these inventions, Kistler Instrument Corporation acquired a worldwide reputation.

Following the sale of Kistler Instrument Corporation in 1970, Walter moved to Seattle, Washington, and, with his partner, Charles Morse, founded Kistler-Morse Corporation. In a development effort spanning several years, Kistler-Morse created the new technology of bolt-on weighing, based on Walter's invention of the Microcell, an extremely sensitive semiconductor strain sensor. Walter subsequently designed and developed a number of additional load cells: load stands, load blocks, and load discs for monitoring the contents of vessels through direct weighing, based on the same innovation. In 1982, he was named an ISA Fellow for his contributions in the field of sensor development. He also became a member of the American National Standards Institute (ANSI) committee that established standards for testing acceleration sensors.

In the 1960s, Walter developed a writing system that he called Steno, derived from German shorthand and adapted to the English language. Having perfected Steno in the subsequent years, Walter initiated a project called The Steno Trust in 1997 to teach the system for applications in education, industry, and law. The most useful application, in Walter's view, is writing diaries.

Over the years, Walter has played a key role in the startup of several high-technology companies either as a Director or as Chairman. These companies include Kistler Products, SRS, ICI, Interpoint, Paroscientific, and SPACEHAB, Inc. In 1993 he co-founded Kistler Aerospace Corporation (Kirkland, WA) to pursue his lifelong dream of designing and building a totally reusable space vehicle. The company is developing the world's first reusable launch vehicles to reduce the cost of access to space by 80 to 90 percent. The reusable system will be capable of launching Earth satellites into low Earth orbit, medium Earth orbit, geosynchronous orbit, and even on escape trajectories to the moon and the planets.

But despite all this technical activity and intense interest in space, there was always in the back of Walter's mind a concern about where humanity was headed.

"When I consider what has happened in the years since I was a boy," he said, "we have deciphered the genetic code and are now able to study the innermost structure of a human being. We have invented the transistor and have developed a computer-based civilization replete with computer games and interactive television. We have even conquered space and humans have walked on the moon. However, few people are aware of the most drastic development that has taken place in humanity's condition, a development of portentous consequences. From the status of a child or teenager, humanity suddenly became an adult in the 20th century. Science and technology have given us so much power that we now control our own destiny. A position of control has its consequences. It entails great responsibility. Unfortunately, we humans don't seem to be aware of this."

This question – how to make people more aware that decisions made by our species now will have binding repercussions on future generations – is the basis of Walter's long-held dream of endowing a foundation that would focus on the very long-term future of the human species. In 1996, the dream took physical form with the establishment of the Foundation For the Future, a private, non-profit foundation dedicated to the purpose of promoting scholarly research to better understand the factors that may have a major impact on the quality of human life during coming millennia.

To put it in Walter's own words: "My feeling is that humanity is like a blind man running around in a dark cave. He is very likely to hit a hard wall and be seriously damaged. The purpose of this foundation is to bring some light into the dark cave and some vision to the blind person in the cave, so that humanity really sees and understands its surroundings, its own essence. Only after there is full understanding and agreement, only then should any action be taken."

Walter Kistler is a life member of the Swiss Physical Society and a member of AIAA and ISA, which presented him the Life Achievement Award in 2000. He is listed in *American Men of Science, Who's Who in Aviation, Who's Who in Finance and Industry,* and *Who's Who in the World.* He is the owner of more than fifty US and foreign patents and the author of a number of papers published in scientific and trade journals.

WALTER KISTLER PHOTO GALLERY

1. Walter Kistler's parents, shown here in 1912, were Hermann and Marguerite (Jeanneret) Kistler.

2. Walter, far right, and his cousin Renée with Walter's Uncle Ben, in 1920.

3. Walter at age six, in 1924.

4. In 1932, after much persuading, Walter, age 14, finally agreed to have his portrait taken professionally by a friend's mother at her studio.

5. Walter, left, was a member of the Swiss Army at age 21, with a continuing obligation until age 35, as required for Swiss male citizens. He is shown here in 1939 with his cousin Jurg.

1. Sylvia, daughter of Walter and Olga, was christened in 1962 at the Methodist Church in Buffalo, NY.

2. Walter and Sylvia celebrate Christmas in 1966 at home in Buffalo, NY.

3. Family portrait taken in 1972 in Seattle when Sylvia was ten years old.

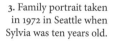

1. Olga and Walter visited Machu Pichu, Peru, in 1980.

2. A happily married couple: Walter and Olga in their home in Redmond, WA, in 1980.

3. Approximately 120 guests attended the wedding when Sylvia married Andrew Thompson in 1990 in Glion, Lake Geneva, Switzerland. Walter, in top hat, gave away the bride.

1. Walter climbed the Matterhorn, in the Swiss Alps, in July 1986, at age 68 (though he reported his age as 58 so that the guide would permit him to make the climb).

2. Walter caught this large salmon in Ketchikan, Alaska, in 1991.

3. Walter attends to camp cooking during a 1993 sailing trip in Desolation Sound, Canada.

1

2

3

1. Key executives of Kistler Instrument Corp., Buffalo, NY, in 1969. STANDING, left to right: Tom Michaels, VP Finance, and Jim Raab, VP Sales & Marketing. SEATED: Bill Waytena, VP Mfg.; Walter Kistler; and Vern Siegel, VP Engineering.

2. In October 1983, Walter, left, and Jerry Paros were honored at the Instrument Society of America (ISA) Convention in Houston, TX. Walter's award recognized his development of quartz instruments and the special system used to test the Apollo vehicle.

3. The European sales representatives of the Kistler-Morse Corp. gathered in 1990 in the Kistler-Morse office in Antwerp, Belgium.

1. A painting by Pat Rawlings, 1994, captures Walter's design for a fully reusable rocket in blast off.

2. Walter points out details of this model of his two-stage reusable rocket at Kistler Aerospace Corporation offices in Kirkland, WA, in 1994.

3. Walter (left) and Bob Citron look over a demonstrator second-stage of Walter's reusable rocket design at Scaled Composites, Mojave, CA, in 1995.

1

4. Walter explains the workings of his reusable rocket in a 1995 meeting at Scaled Composites offices, Mojave, CA.

3

5. Computer-generated rendering of the Kistler Aerospace K-1 rocket design in lift-off, 1996.

2

6. The Kistler Aerospace Corporation staff, shown in 1995 at offices in Kirkland, WA. Dr. George Mueller (STANDING, far left) became CEO in 1995. Walter Kistler (STANDING, far right) and Bob Citron (SEATED, far right) co-founded Kistler Aerospace.

4

5

6

1

2

3

4

5

1. Foundation For the Future trustees at the Kistler Prize Banquet in 2002. Left to right: Sesh Velamoor, Deputy Director; Bob Citron, Executive Director; Donna Hines, Deputy Director; Walter Kistler, Founder; and Milt Woods, Trustee.

2. Painter Robert McCall created the Foundation For the Future mural in 1998. The mural is displayed at the Foundation's headquarters in Bellevue, WA. It depicts the progression from the origin of the universe to the far future.

3. Bob Citron and Walter Kistler, pictured in front of the McCall mural, celebrate at the inauguration of the Foundation For the Future in 1998.

4. Foundation For the Future office building, Bellevue, WA.

5. In 2002, Walter received a surprise present from Veronica Spencer, leader of the Steno project: the prototype copy of *The Steno Textbook*, which is used to teach a writing system developed for the English language by Walter after his move to the United States. Most of Walter's diaries, written over six decades, were written in Steno.

1. The Kistler Prize emblem, designed in 2000. The Prize includes a cash award of US$100,000 and is awarded annually to recognize original contributions to the understanding of the connection between human heredity and human society.

2. Walter announces Dr. E.O. Wilson of Harvard University as the first recipient of the Kistler Prize, at the Kistler Prize Banquet and Ceremony, Seattle, WA, August 15, 2000.

3, 4. Before a gathering of 200 guests, Walter lifts the Kistler Prize gold medallion for 2000 from its glass sculpture and presents it to Dr. E.O. Wilson.

5. Each Kistler Prize medallion is accompanied by a display mounting, a glass sculpture representing the Matterhorn in the Swiss Alps.

6. Dr. E.O. Wilson accepts the first Kistler Prize from Walter Kistler.

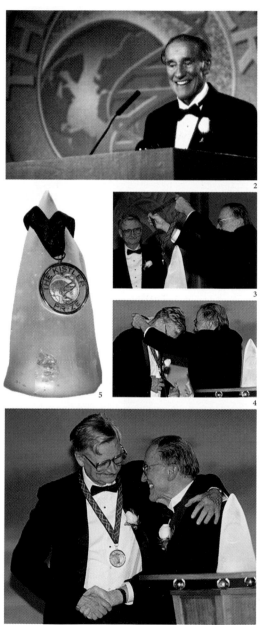

ABOUT THE FOUNDATION FOR THE FUTURE

THE FOUNDATION FOR THE FUTURE is a private, non-profit foundation endowed in 1996 to increase and diffuse knowledge concerning the long-term future of humanity. It is led by Walter Kistler, its founder and President, and supported by a Board of Trustees, an Executive Director (Bob Citron), two Deputy Directors (Sesh Velamoor and Donna Hines), and a small administrative staff. Guidance is regularly sought from the Foundation's Board of Advisors, a distinguished international panel of 14 scholars and scientists. Additional panels of advisors have been created to assist the Foundation in the overall direction of three key programs: Humanity 3000, *The Next Thousand Years* television series, and the Kistler Prize

Foundation programs are described below. In all its endeavors, the Foundation is dedicated to serving its mission.

HUMANITY 3000

The most visible program of the Foundation is Humanity 3000, established in 1998 and designed to bring together at regular intervals a changing roster of some of the world's most prominent thinkers. The purpose of these conferences is to assess the current state of humanity and to identify the most significant factors that may affect the quality of life for the people of the Earth in the next thousand years. Participants in Humanity 3000's annual seminars and bidecadal symposia come from around the world to take part in the multidisciplinary dialogues focused on the question: "Where does humanity go from here?"

At its first symposium, held in August 2000, 70 scholars from 40 intellectual and professional disciplines and 20 countries gathered in Seattle as guests of the Foundation. The annual seminars typically convene 25 participants. In addition, smaller workshops are conducted as needed to provide a knowledge base for seminar and symposia participants.

Such assemblies of scholars from different worldviews, different countries, and different fields of learning mean that there is wide variance of opinion expressed in the meetings. "It should be noted that it is neither avoidable nor objectionable when researchers and experts strongly disagree on a subject," said Walter Kistler. "In fact, it is a good sign. It shows their concern and will get people to work harder on solutions."

The Foundation is very clear that it is not a proponent of any particular course of action, nor is it an advocate for any cause or position beyond its mission to increase and diffuse knowledge concerning the long-term future of humanity. It endeavors to provide a forum in which all viewpoints and opinions can be heard.

THE KISTLER PRIZE

An important element of Walter Kistler's earliest vision for the Foundation was an award program to recognize and reward original contributions to the understanding of the connection between human heredity and human society – especially those contributions stemming from research conducted with courage and conviction despite opposition from peers or the public. These contributions must be of a scientific nature, employing scientific methods to establish the connections between heredity and human behavior.

In 1999, this element of the vision was realized with the establishment of the annual Kistler Prize, consisting of a US$100,000 cash award and a specially designed 180-gram gold medallion. Nominees may be either individuals or research institutions, from anywhere in the world.

Three recipients of the Kistler Prize have been named so far. In 2000, the first awarding of the Prize was to Dr. Edward O. Wilson, Pellegrino University Research Professor and Honorary Curator of Entomology at Harvard University. The work for which Dr. Wilson received the Prize is the introduction of biological thought into the social sciences and humanities to create a new field called sociobiology. Dr. Wilson defined sociobiology as the systematic study of the biological basis of all forms of social behavior in humans as well as other life forms.

The 2001 recipient of the Kistler Prize was Dr. Richard Dawkins, Oxford University zoologist, Darwinist, and evolutionary biologist. The Prize recognized Dr. Dawkins' work in the ethology of the gene, work that redirected the focus of the "levels of selection" debate away from the individual animal as the unit of evolution to the genes and their extended phenotypes. At the same time, he applied a Darwinian view to culture through the concept of memes as replicators of culture. Both the gene and the meme, said Dr. Dawkins, are replicators that mutate and compete in parallel and interacting struggles for their own propagation.

The winner of the 2002 Kistler Prize was Luigi Luca Cavalli-Sforza, M.D., Professor of Genetics Emeritus (active), Stanford Medical School, and world-renowned expert on human genetic diversity. Dr. Cavalli-Sforza has traced historical migrations by analyzing the genetic differences between humans living today, employing genetics as well as multiple other disciplines to track 100,000 years of human and cultural evolution. He was one of the founders of, and continues in the work of, the Human Genome Diversity Project, aimed at accumulating DNA samples from populations all over the world for a comprehensive study of human genetic difference.

Each year the Kistler Prize is presented personally by Walter Kistler at a formal banquet and ceremony in Seattle. Invited guests include distinguished academic, business, and political leaders.

THE WALTER P. KISTLER BOOK AWARD

The Foundation For the Future established a new prize in 2003, the Walter P. Kistler Book Award, to recognize authors who make important contributions to the public's understanding of the factors that may impact the long-term future of humanity. The Award includes a cash prize of US$10,000 and a certificate. It will be awarded annually to authors of science-based books that significantly increase the knowledge and understanding of the public regarding subjects that will shape the future of our species.

Such books are critical to the human future because scientific and technological advances will continue to create possibilities beyond current human imagination.

These possibilities may radically alter the evolution of societies, politics, religions, cultures – even what it means to be *human*. They are certain to have an impact on what will become of the human species. The public must be informed about these advances and their implications in order to make appropriate decisions as events unfold.

The first recipient of the Walter P. Kistler Book Award was Dr. Gregory Stock, Director of the Program on Medicine, Technology, and Society at the School of Public Health, University of California at Los Angeles, for his book *Redesigning Humans: Our Inevitable Genetic Future* (Houghton Mifflin, 2002). Dr. Stock is an expert in the implications of scientific advances in reproductive biology. *Redesigning Humans* explicates the enhancement technologies that will enable parents to make choices about their children's appearance, capabilities, and health risks.

THE NEXT THOUSAND YEARS TELEVISION SERIES

An outgrowth of the Foundation's Humanity 3000 program is a four-program documentary series for public television entitled *The Next Thousand Years*, now in project planning. The programs are expected to air in 2006.

Advances in understanding in scientific fields as varied as genetics, cosmology, medicine, nanotechnology, robotics, biology, and ecology continue to push back the frontiers of knowledge. These advances are allowing humankind to project trends and speculate about the future with a greater degree of confidence than ever before. Starting with an informative grounding in the latest relevant developments in these scientific fields, the programs in the series will present a rational approach to examining the various alternative futures that might be possible. Is this prediction? "You cannot predict the future," said Walter Kistler, "but certainly you know the trends that have existed for billions of years for more complex things to evolve from unicellular life. You see what the trends have been, and the trends are likely to continue with incremental modifications."

Developments in genetics promise a future in which humans directly influence their own evolution, gain a deeper understanding of life and human origins, and learn more about what is immutable in human nature and what is changeable. As these developments emerge, the future will be strongly influenced by the decisions humankind makes about them. The purposes of this television series are to help an informed public engage with the drivers of change, to understand the catastrophic events that threaten humanity's survival, to explore the moral and ethical issues surrounding choices, and to examine humankind's ability – and responsibility – to manage the species' future. All programs in the series will utilize the work and visions of some of the most prominent thinkers of today.

More than 75 scientists, social scientists, and other scholars from around the world have agreed to participate in the development of *The Next Thousand Years* television series. The Foundation convened in April 2002 the first Producers Workshop to enable scholars and television documentary producers to discuss the content of the programs and how to create an effective, educational, and entertaining television series. A subsequent workshop in

November 2002 focused on the content of the program "The Future Human." Additional workshops will be conducted to discuss content for the remaining programs: "This Tiny Planet," "The Evolution of Culture," and "The Horizons on Knowledge."

An extensive Educational Outreach Program is also planned in connection with the television series.

CENTER FOR HUMAN EVOLUTION

The Foundation established the Center for Human Evolution in 1998 with the primary objective of convening prominent thinkers from pertinent fields in small, informal workshops to share their knowledge and perspectives of the evolutionary factors affecting the long-term future of humanity.

Two early workshops on the evolution of human intelligence were attended by distinguished scholars from the such diverse fields as neurophysiology, genetics, philosophy, astrophysics, medicine, biological anthropology, and psychology. Subsequent Center for Human Evolution workshops have focused on cultural evolution and how evolution works. Five to six scholars have participated in each workshop.

Each participant prepares a position paper for presentation and discussion during the workshop, and each gathering of scholars also addresses specific questions developed by the Foundation to explore details and ramifications of the workshop topic.

Research Grant Awards

The Foundation's research grant awards program provides financial support to scholars, either individuals or organizations, to undertake research directly related to a better understanding of the factors affecting quality of life for the long-term future of humanity.

Preliminary Grant Applications, available on the Foundation's website, must be completed in English by potential grantees and accepted by the Foundation prior to submission of full proposals. Research grants – and the other activities supported by the Foundation – have no political, social, geographic, or cultural boundaries.

Education and Outreach

The Education and Outreach program undertakes public awareness concerning the long-term future of the human species. It includes financial support for educational workshops, films, and websites; papers delivered at futures conferences; and visits by Foundation staff and Foundation-event participants to schools and other organizations.

To support the teaching and understanding of science, evolution, and future studies, the Foundation has financially supported the Futures Research wing of the OECD and the United Nations University's Millennium Committee. Foundation staff have also routinely written and delivered papers for future study-oriented organizations such as Tamkang University (Taipei), the World Future Studies Federation, and The World Future Society.

The Foundation's first science educators workshop was held in 1999, gathering two dozen of the top science teachers and science professors from all over the United States at the University of Washington for an intensive workshop emphasizing the teaching of evolution and the nature of science.

In 2002, the Foundation sponsored and awarded the first annual NABT Evolution Education Award, in conjunction with the National Association of Biology Teachers. The award was established to recognize innovative and effective classroom teaching and community education to promote the accurate understanding of biological evolution. It included $1,000 in cash plus travel expenses to the NABT convention and a plaque.

In conjunction with the first awarding of the Walter P. Kistler Book Award in 2003, the Foundation initiated a student essay contest open to students in two categories, high school and below, and college and above. The essay topic was: "What are the implications of genetic enhancement technologies for our long-term future?" A total of $600 in cash awards was paid to contest winners.

An extensive Educational Outreach Program, planned in connection with *The Next Thousand Years* television series, will feature a comprehensive website with an array of free educational and professional-development resources aimed at a general audience, including interactive games, online expeditions and interviews, and animated narratives. It will also seek to transform the way science and technology are taught and learned in schools throughout the United States by providing teachers with resources that expand their content knowledge, including an online digital library and downloadable teacher training, all emphasizing strong interdisciplinary connections.

Deputy Director Sesh Velamoor makes annual visits to a Bellevue, Washington, classroom for students of high academic potential, and regularly speaks on radio and to groups. He is available to speak to any organization that is interested in thinking about issues related to the long-term future of humanity.

An important element of the Foundation's public awareness and education programs is educating young people about how the choices they make in their own lives may affect the future of humankind.

VIDEOS AND DVDS

In addition to the programs and activities described above, the Foundation develops video productions and sponsors the production of films aimed at increasing and diffusing knowledge concerning the long-term future of humanity.

The 15-minute film *Cosmic Origins: From the Big Bang to Humanity* was produced in 2000 by Palfreman Film Group for the Foundation For the Future and the Wright Center for Science Education at Tufts University. This film has been distributed in video format to more than 5,000 classrooms across the United States. It will soon be available as streaming video from the Foundation's website at www.futurefoundation.org.

The 13-minute video *Where Does Humanity Go from Here?* synopsizes the Foundation's work with leading scientists, academicians, philosophers, and futurists in discussion about humanity's long-term future. This film is updated annually by the Foundation.

A 12-minute film of the first Kistler Prize Award Ceremony, featuring highlights of the presentation of the Kistler Prize to Dr. Edward O. Wilson of Harvard University and his acceptance, was produced in 2000.

Also captured on video footage are keynote addresses by Philip Tobias, Leroy Hood, Crispin Tickell, Ervin Laszlo, Michio Kaku, Ronald Bailey, William Calvin, Johan Galtung, Lui Lam, Michael Shermer, Peter Ward, and Gregory Stock. Captured on audiotape are interviews by Sesh Velamoor with Jerome Glenn and Francis Heylighen, Christian de Duve and Crispin Tickell, Michio Kaku and Ervin Laszlo, and Richard Dawkins and Norman Levitt. The Foundation also videotapes key portions of all Humanity 3000 seminars and symposia.

Visions of the Thousand-Year Future, featuring scholar interviews, is in production for release in 2004.

PUBLICATIONS

The Foundation's Publications Program publishes proceedings of Foundation seminars, symposia, and workshops, including transcripts of all discussion sessions. Proceedings volumes and reports, listed below, are downloadable from the Foundation's website. Many volumes are also available in print editions.

- *Humanity 3000 Seminar No. 3 Proceedings* (2003)
- *The Next Thousand Years Television Series: The Future Human Workshop* (2003)

- *The Next Thousand Years Television Series: First Producers Workshop Report* (2002)
- *Humanity 3000 Symposium No. 1 Proceedings,* two volumes, also available on CD-ROM (2001)
- *Humanity 3000 Seminar No. 2 Proceedings* (2000)
- *When SETI Succeeds: The Impact of High-Information Contact,* edited by Dr. Allen Tough (2000)
- *The Evolution of Human Intelligence,* combined proceedings of two Center for Human Evolution workshops (2000)
- *Humanity 3000 Seminar No. 1 Proceedings* (1999)

In addition, the Foundation regularly publishes newsletters, brochures, and other printed and media materials on the future of humanity.

FUTURE STUDIES LIBRARY

Finally, the Foundation boasts a diverse and unique collection of books, tapes, and journals approaching 3,000 volumes, unlikely to be duplicated anywhere else, for facilitation of the study and understanding of the long-term future of humanity. Library resources are available for use by the public.

A VISION IN PERPETUITY

Walter Kistler's vision is still unfolding. In fact, essential components of his vision will be unfolding for centuries. Every program of the Foundation is orchestrated with a long-term view. For example, the Humanity 3000 program is designed with the expectation that such meetings of prominent thinkers will continue annually for coming millennia, with each meeting casting its collective mind a thousand years into the future. And existing recognition plaques for Kistler Prize recipients have room for over 250 years' worth of awardees' names.

"Today it is no longer Nature but ourselves who rule the ways and the direction of humanity's development," said Walter Kistler. "Now there is a question: How will we humans handle what Nature has handled up till now? Will we make a mess out of it or will we be able to handle it? What can we do to ensure that we don't mishandle it?"

These are questions that are applicable whether the issue is the environment or species diversity or human reproduction or world population or the planet's ecology, as well as such emerging issues as artificial intelligence, human augmentation, nanotechnology, and genomics. Walter Kistler's ongoing vision is that the Foundation For the Future will continue to encourage knowledge – both its production and diffusion – so that people all over the world, now and long into the future, will intelligently, thoughtfully consider the questions: "Where does humanity go from here? Will we take responsibility for the role we play in the answer to that question?"

FOUNDATION FOR THE FUTURE
123 105th Avenue SE
Bellevue, WA 98004
425-451-1333
EMAIL: info@futurefoundation.org
WEBSITE: www.futurefoundation.org

ABOUT FRANK MIELE

FRANK MIELE is the author of *Intelligence, Race, and Genetics: Conversations with Arthur R. Jensen* (Boulder, CO: Westview Press, 2002) and *The Battlegrounds of Bio-Science: Cross-Examining the Experts on: Evolutionary Psychology; Race, Intelligence, & Genetics; Population, Environment, & Cloning* (Bloomington, IN: 1st Books Library, 2002), a collection of his *Skeptic* Magazine articles summarizing the opposing viewpoints on scientific issues and interviewing world-class scholars, including Kistler Prize winners E.O. Wilson and Richard Dawkins.

Miele's *Skeptic* article "The (Im)moral Animal: A Quick and Dirty Guide to Evolutionary Psychology & the Nature of Human Nature" was selected to appear on *Human Behavior and Evolution Society* (HBES) and other websites, and named a Best Web Site Resource by *The Encyclopedia Britannica On-line*. He has been interviewed on National Public Radio's *Science Friday* and *Forum*.

In addition to *Skeptic* Magazine, Miele has published in *Intelligence, The Human Ethology Bulletin*, and *Population and Environment*. His unique writing style, drawing upon his varied life experience, combines a technical writer's accuracy, brevity, and clarity, a musician's ear for catching the rhythm, style, and personality of his iconoclastic and bestselling interviewees, and the wry wit of a stand-up comic.

INDEX